Praise for

"Gilder's originality, plus the sheer force of his enthusiasm for the extraordinary virtues of the beleaguered Jewish state, sweep away the prevailing vitriol and make for a book that is nothing less than thrilling to read."

—Norman Podhoretz

"*The Israel Test* spoke to me with unexpected power. Apart from being brilliantly, fiercely written, its merit lies in clarifying, in a totally new, secular, and intuitive way, why Israel matters."

—David Klinghoffer, *The Jerusalem Post*

"In *The Israel Test*, George Gilder fights back, refuting the hateful lies and slanders that are all too frequently hurled at Israel. Gilder argues convincingly that Israel's future is ultimately inseparable from the future of freedom and democracy everywhere. Israel embodies the ideals and principles that define the United States and our best allies worldwide: the values of personal liberty and economic freedom, human rights and women's rights, tolerance and pluralism."

—Senator Joseph Leiberman

"George Gilder has written a superlative defense of capitalism and how it relates to Israel becoming the world's most advanced nation in the development of the new technologies, second only to the United States. Tiny Israel, barely the size of New Jersey, with a population of more than seven million, now has more brain power than all of Europe."

—Dr. Samuel Blumenfeld, WorldNetDaily

THE
ISRAEL
TEST

How Israel's Genius Enriches
and Challenges the World

GEORGE GILDER

New York · London

First American edition published in 2009 by Encounter Books,
an activity of Encounter for Culture and Education, Inc.,
a nonprofit, tax-exempt corporation.
Encounter Books website address: www.encounterbooks.com

Manufactured in the United States and printed on
acid-free paper. The paper used in this publication meets
the minimum requirements of ANSI/NISO Z39.48-1992
(R 1997) (*Permanence of Paper*).

SECOND AMERICAN PAPERBACK EDITION

LIBRARY OF CONGRESS CATALOGING-IN-PUBLICATION DATA IS AVAILABLE

Information for this title can be found at the Library of Congress
website under the following ISBN 978-1-64177-427-7 and LCCN 2024023669.

For Anne Mandelbaum, who reshaped this book

CONTENTS

FOREWORD

By Dennis Prager

As counterintuitive as it may sound, the most prescient books on the Jews have frequently been written by non-Jews. Apparently, outsiders often see things more clearly than those about whom they write. To cite the most famous example, it was a Frenchman, Alexis de Tocqueville, who wrote what is generally deemed the most insightful book about America in the nineteenth century, and perhaps about America at any time.

I would place George Gilder and this book, *The Israel Test*, in that rare category. No living writer understands the Jews and Israel—and the world's reactions to the Jews and Israel—better than he does. Which is why the publication of a new edition of *The Israel Test* is of such importance—particularly at this moment.

At the time I am writing these words, Israel, one of the world's most decent societies, has become the world's pariah state. This would be impossible in a decent world. But the world is not decent. Its moral compass is broken; and, as has almost always been the case, when that compass breaks its brokenness is first revealed with regard to the Jews.

As has often been noted, the Jews—and now the Jewish state—are the proverbial canaries in the coal mine. Miners would take canaries down into the mines because canaries succumb to noxious fumes before human beings do. So, when miners saw the canaries die, they understood that they must either fight those fumes or get out of the mine.

Applying the analogy to the outside world, the canaries are the Jews and the miners are everyone else. Incredibly, however, unlike miners, when non-Jews see Jews dying most do not recognize that they, too, are in peril—that there are noxious fumes to be fought. Most non-Jews assume either the canaries did something that caused them to die, or the fumes that killed the canaries only target canaries and won't kill them. Thus, the non-Jewish world dismissed Nazism as the Jews' problem—a mistake that cost tens of millions non-Jewish lives and shattered a continent.

The world's reaction to today's Nazis—Hamas (and Hezbollah, both proxies of the Jew-hating theocracy in Iran)—is a repeat. Hamas is dismissed as a problem for the Jews and Israel, and not the problem of non-Jews, nor a threat to Western civilization. Indeed, among Western elites, the prevailing view is that Israel had the events of October 7th coming. What else should an occupier, colonizer, and apartheid state expect? It just stands to reason that its citizens will be burned alive, family by family; its women raped, tortured, mutilated, and murdered; its babies and grandparents kidnapped and taken hostage.

Gilder perfectly summarizes Israel-hatred (and Jew-hatred): "Israel is hated above all for its virtues."

That is why the more morally corrupt the Israel-hater, the greater the hatred. The greater the moral gap between Israel and any group, the more that group will hate Israel. When I describe Hamas as today's Nazis, I am not attacking Hamas; I am describing it. Hamas, like the Nazis, seeks the annihilation of the Jewish people—individually, and as embodied in the Jewish state. The only identifiable difference between Hamas and the Nazis is that the Nazis tried to hide their atrocities, while Hamas proudly videoed theirs.

As for Israel's virtues, it has everything Hamas and the Palestinians do not: free elections, a robust, free, and critical press, an independent judiciary, human rights groups, women's rights, and gay rights. It also has two million Arab citizens who have every civil right Israeli Jews have. Israel's Arabs are the freest Arabs in the Middle East. They even have their own political parties.

And while on the subject of Israel's virtues, I call the reader's attention to two moral assessments of Israel's army, the IDF.

The first is that of Colonel Richard Kemp, the commander of British Forces in Afghanistan: "The Israel Defense Force, the IDF, does more to safeguard the rights of civilians in a combat zone than any other army in the history of warfare.... Judaism, with its unsurpassed moral standards, remains a major influence on the citizens of Israel. I say this as a non-Jew." Watch his five-minute video, "Israel: The World's Most Moral Army," online at PragerU.

The second was written by John Spencer, chair of urban warfare studies at the Modern War Institute at West Point, the American military academy. It was published in *Newsweek* four months into the Israel-Hamas war. "Israel has implemented more measures to prevent civilian casualties than any other military in history.... In fact, as someone who has served two tours in Iraq and studied urban warfare for over a decade, Israel has taken precautionary measures even the United States did not do during its recent wars in Iraq and Afghanistan."

Israel's decency is why Hamas hates Israel and the Jews. It is the reason why that amoral institution, the United Nations—which is, of course, nothing more than the United Governments—has passed more resolutions condemning Israel than any other nation in the world.

Evil hates good. The miserable hate the happy. The failures hate the successes. Tyrants hate free societies (which is, to cite another example, why China hates Taiwan and squashed tiny Hong Kong).

That is why *The Israel Test*—both the book and the test itself—so clearly explains the world in which we live.

I wish it weren't so.

Dennis Prager is the co-founder of PragerU and author of Why the Jews? The Reason for Antisemitism, the Greatest Predictor of Evil *and* The Rational Bible, *a five-volume commentary on the Torah, the first five books of the Bible.*

13 FEBRUARY, 2024

On a visit to Israel more than a decade ago my long-time friend and editor Richard Vigilante bought a tee-shirt inscribed with the slogan, "Don't Worry America, Israel is Behind You." As he recalls, the street vendor, handing him the shirt with a shy and ironic smile, confessed, "I know—it's really the other way around, isn't it?"

Surely not. As I prepare a new edition of this venerable book, I find that its central message is as enduring as ever. In the throes of the twenty-first century, we Americans still face our Israel Test, our humbling need not only to recognize our dependence on the genius of the Jews in the United States, but also to acknowledge our reliance not only for innovation but even for our national security on this diminutive and embattled Middle Eastern ally. As when I wrote the first edition of the book a quarter century ago, no nation is more important to the survival of the United States and the world than Israel.

The panoply of Israeli companies that fuel the American economy with innovation may vary from decade to decade with mergers, acquisitions, relocations in the US, and occasional attrition. But America's reliance on Israel has only increased as the years have passed and as our economy has slipped into a bureaucratic slough, fraught with the delusional agenda of climate-change socialism, intrinsically anti-Semitic and anti-Asian diversity, equity, and inclusion (DEI) regulations, and the related deterioration of our leading universities.

It is not only that most of America's preeminent technology companies, from Intel to IBM, from Google to Qualcomm, and its healthcare giants from Johnson & Johnson to Pfizer, still depend on crucial inventors, engineers, intellectual property and laboratories in Israel. But Israeli innovations, from drones to battlefield artificial intelligence to a world-leading complex of cyber security companies, have changed the very nature of warfare. To meet the challenge, we must recognize the deterioration of our woke, sclerotic, and vastly expensive military. Our increasingly baroque and Brobdingnagian weapons systems, like giant aircraft carriers, missiles, and battle tanks linked to GPS, render us an increasingly vulnerable Goliath. We can benefit from Israel's innovations that like David's slingshot of old yield unexpected coups and adapt our defenses to twenty-first century forms of warfare.

Instead, what we find in the United States is not the immense gratitude that Israel deserves but an insidious spate of abusive nonsense detailing the alleged *flaws*—indeed the *sins*—of Israel. Having built the world's preeminent high-tech economy on a mere 4 percent of Middle Eastern territory, Israel is denounced from continental America as somehow too "big." Even staunch Israel supporters tend to bend over backwards to concede that Israel deserves "intense criticism" for much of its behavior. With a per-capita income, among Jews and Arab citizens alike, higher than overall earnings in Germany, France, the UK, or Japan, Israel is alleged to exploit Arab labor. But Israeli Arabs are the richest population of Arabs in the world, comprising 21 percent of Israel's population. Nearly twenty thousand Arabs work in high-tech companies, many with engineering jobs.

Although Israel withdrew from Gaza in 2004, Israel is nonetheless ludicrously described by its critics as an "occupier," an "imperialist" power dedicated to a nefarious predatory vision of a "Greater Israel." Israelis are said to "settle" on contiguous land, "occupying" the "West Bank" (Judaea and Samaria) by paying again and again for the land with their blood and treasure and making it bloom as never before, employing eight Arabs for every "settler."

As war raged in Gaza in early 2024, *Harper's* magazine emblazoned on its cover a jeremiad by the Israeli-American Bernard Avishai indulging in all these canards. Then he added his own precious memories of Jewish secular labor Zionism that had somehow been betrayed in subsequent years, mostly by regimes linked to Benjamin Netanyahu. He failed to see that Israeli leftism, like leftism everywhere, was nothing short of a life-threatening disaster for Israel, leading the country into an abyss, as it perilously approached 1,000 percent inflation in 1985. Israel survived because of Netanyahu's redemptive supply-side fiscal leadership and his welcome of one million refugees from the Soviet Union, many of them scientists and software engineers and all passionately anti-socialist. Electing and reelecting Netanyahu, they saved the State of Israel from likely destruction. Totalling only 16 percent of Israel's population, its Soviet immigrants soon came to comprise an astounding one-half the employees of Israel's high-tech businesses.

Avishai concluded with an invidious coda of moral equivalence between "both peoples" (Israelis and Palestinians, each supposedly dedicated to the removal of the other). Since Arabs flourish in Israel as they do nowhere else, with greater wealth, longevity, and personal freedoms, while Jews have been banished from nearly all the lands that comprise the remaining 96 percent of the Middle East, this pretense of moral equivalence between jihadists and Jewish settlers from such an eminent scholar is fatuous if not depraved.

Critics of Israel forget that the country emerged into statehood not chiefly through US indulgence and support but, on the contrary, through brutal American abandonment. In 1948, despite President Harry Truman's pro-Israel views, the otherwise sainted General George Marshall, Truman's secretary of state from 1947-1949, banned all US sales of military equipment to Israel. The British Labor government of Clement Attlee followed suit. Pentagon authorities expected the nascent nation to be strangled in its cradle. Scrounging weapons from Czechoslovakia and other kindred European outcasts, Israel survived by its own military resourcefulness and world-leading technological savvy.

Even though the US has given Israel crucial backing from time to time—notably under the presidencies of Richard Nixon during the 1973 Yom Kippur War and, more recently, Donald Trump—we have compromised our aid with our hopelessly counterproductive insistence on a "peace process" and its related deeply deleterious "two-state solution." Through the so-called UN Relief and Works Agency for Palestinian Refugees (UNRWA), we have also lavished tens of billions of dollars on Palestinian war aims and jihadist manias. The UNRWA uses billions of US dollars (one billion in 2023 alone) assiduously to cultivate hatred of Israel among its four generations of mostly spurious "refugees." Intractably subversive of Israel and mendacious about Palestinian "refugees" were US Presidents Jimmy Carter and Barack Obama. Even the Bush presidencies were chiefly devoted to their quixotic grand designs in the region and mostly treated Israel as a nuisance or distraction.

The net result of all these policies was to subvert Israel's defense against its *naqba*-obsessed neighbors who in their "shame cultures" see Israel as an intolerable humiliation. Tabulating it over the years, US aid and policy demonstrates a strong bias in favor of Israel's adversaries, in net effect dwarfing the size of US aid for Israel. No American administration until Donald Trump was unabashedly Zionist, as he moved the embassy to Jerusalem and negotiated the Abraham Accords with a number of Arab states. Joseph Biden's subsequent Democratic administration, with the hapless Anthony Blinken as his secretary of state, reverted to the Obama anti-Israel "peace process" and filled its "two-state" Trojan Horse with dollars and duplicity.

Overall, by regarding Israeli power, prosperity, culture, genius, and self-defense as a problem rather than a supreme global asset and human consummation, the United States has all too often failed the Israel Test.

Confronted with an exemplary nation propelled by entrepreneurial creativity and drive, many American intellectuals see only predatory overreach. Confounded by the Marxist "labor theory of value," leftists are blind to the virtue of economic accomplishment through the genius of minuscule minorities. Their theory of value deems the wealthy to be predominantly parasites on labor, scarcely more virtuous than thieves.

As Elon Musk observed in 2023, all too many demand-side thinkers uphold an image of the economy as a "magic horn of plenty" that spontaneously pours forth its bounty. In this prevailing view, various groups vie in a zero-sum war of all-against-all in a selfish effort to direct the flow of "demand" only to themselves. If some get more, others must get less. The winners are deemed oppressors and culpable; the losers are celebrated as presumptively virtuous victims. In this paradigm of victim-virtue, popular in our increasingly demented universities, Israel's manifest success in getting more than its neighbors automatically makes it an oppressor.

All such myopic fantasies fall before Israel's luminous economic achievements, which demonstrably enrich the US and the world. Israeli success requires that we acknowledge that planetary prosperity depends on the outsized genius of a tiny minority of human beings. In Israel's fierce meritocracy, as Edward Luttwak reports in his eye-opening book *The Art of Military Innovation: Lessons From the Israel Defense Forces*, this nation produces a vastly outsized share of the world's innovations from a comparatively tiny minority of creative people. Every year, out of thousands of aspiring "talpions" (elite Israeli Defense Forces, selected solely on merit in the sciences and on their leadership abilities), only forty manage to pass the math and physics requirements and join the group. Yet the graduates from this tiny elite corps and from the similarly famed "Unit 8200"—an IDF force responsible for clandestine operations and signal intelligence—account not only for a wildly disproportionate number of scholarly medals and awards, but also for much of Israel's and the world's entrepreneurial "horns of plenty." By 2023, the number of talpions, for instance, had mounted only to 1,000 in a couple of decades. Yet from such a tiny outpost of merit-based creativity comes much of the wealth of the world.

Today, as I write, the evidence of Israeli technological leadership continues to accumulate. Citing advances in biotechnology, the *Jerusalem Post* reported an announcement in *Nature* of the invention of a new artificial intelligence algorithm called "CUMAb" that enables the conversion of animal antibodies into safe medicines without the laborious random abuse of thousands of immunized horses, guinea pigs, and mice. On the four-man team at the Weitzmann Institute that made the breakthrough was an Arab Israeli named Razi Khalaila. The team leader, Sarel Fleishman, noted that the new method is "likely to become a key element in accelerating the transition from therapeutic candidate molecules to real-world drugs." This kind of intellectual leadership manifests itself continually in Israel's vibrant economy. Israeli companies such as Compugen and Nucleai provide crucial research and intellectual property for pharmaceutical titans around the globe such as AstraZeneca and Johnson & Johnson.

My next book will describe a breakthrough in the field of the material sciences with a likely impact in the twenty-first century comparable to the Industrial Revolution in the nineteenth century or the rise of aluminum and silicon in the twentieth century: the discovery of a two-dimensional sheet of carbon called graphene. The science behind this breakthrough already has garnered five Nobel Prizes and has generated some forty related peer-reviewed papers a day during the seventeen years since it was first widely recognized. Two-hundred times stronger than steel, as flexible as rubber, a thousand times more conductive than copper, and the best transmitter of heat ever discovered, graphene resembles diamonds that can be manufactured from garbage or plastic waste. It will transform every industry from electronics and healthcare to the power grid and space travel (NASA has declared that it is needed in "every part of the space program").

Major graphene breakthroughs have come from a laboratory at Rice University in Houston run by chemistry prodigy, James Tour. But when his students sought to form companies to pursue their transformative ideas, Tour discovered that American venture capitalists, preoccupied with software and AI, were indifferent. "I would have to teach them organic chemistry," he commented. Of the total of eighteen companies emerging from his laboratory—devoted to new memory technologies, new batteries, new methods for DNA sequencing, new cures for Downs Syndrome and pancreatic cancer, new ways to repair severed spinal cords, and new forms of nanorobotics—seventeen finally found life-saving funds and manpower in Israel.

Blinding the world to Israel's supreme accomplishments are the same economic statisticians who also obscure the sources of all real economic growth. As the Yale Nobel Laureate William Nordhaus has shown, official economic data vastly underestimate the contributions of ingenious innovators to the wealth of nations.

Studying the history of lighting through the centuries—from the cave fires of the Neanderthals, to the candles at Versailles, and to whale oil, kerosene, and the Edison's lightbulb, and finishing with fluorescence and light emitting diodes—the Yale scholar found that economic data missed almost all of it. Measuring progress through the universal metric of time-prices—how many hours and minutes workers had to spend to gain the wherewithal to purchase goods and services—he found relatively scant gains over the millennia before the Industrial Revolution. Then everything changed and progress exploded on an exponential path. But most of these gains eluded the statisticians.

Despite this ascent of ever more efficient lighting illuminating the night, economic analysis remains shrouded in an idiom of "dark satanic mills," "exploitation," and other images from the dismal science. Many official statistics convey a Malthusian vision of scarcity, with each additional human deemed a new burden on the planet. Humans are deemed chiefly as mouths—consumers of resources—rather than as the minds that create them.

As Gale Pooley and Marian Tupy document in their revelatory tome, *Superabundance*, the Nordhaus insight on the time-prices of lighting applies across the entire private economy. Extending time prices from lighting to all goods and commodities, Tupy and Pooley show that since World War II real economic growth has occurred at rates at least twice as fast as those measured by economists. Since 1980, for example, the global population nearly doubled from 4.4 billion to eight billion, but measured by time-prices the cost of the fifty major commodities sustaining human life plummeted some 75 percent. As Pooley and Tupy show, almost everything in the private sector became—simultaneously—less costly and more abundant.

While economists obsess about rising prices in an inflationary era, Tupy and Pooley demonstrated that real prices have, in fact, plummeted as measured by time. While measures of GDP valued government spending at cost, despite its manifest waste and widespread counterproductive bureaucracies, GDP numbers radically underestimated productivity and innovation in the private sector.

As the world's most innovative country, with redemptive public-sector spending on defense technology, Israel by the time-price gauge, grew an estimated two times faster even than the per-capita income measures surpassing Germany, the UK, France, and Japan. It was a stunning economic miracle.

Amazingly, Israel's economic miracle occurred in the face of a series of invasions, intifadas, missile attacks, and other assaults by its neighbors, from the wars of 1948 and 1967, through the Yom Kippur War in 1973, to the Hamas atrocities and the accompanying Hezbollah missiles of October 2023. Propelled by its innovations in weapons systems, Israel repeatedly made zero-to-one breakthroughs—in Peter Thiel's vivid phrase—such as drones and anti-missiles, which mitigated the effects of the brutality and the element of surprise of its jihadist assailants. Israel's achievement is deeply relevant to the defense of the United States, which focuses on elaborating and embellishing existing systems with diminishing returns that potential enemies already understand and can counter. If there should ever occur an all-out missile attack against the US, Israeli technology will be the reason we will likely survive it.

Indeed, as documented by my colleague Richard Vigilante, Israel's advances have made such an attack increasingly improbable. Not only the US, but every nation on earth, will owe Israel a debt of gratitude for its key contributions to the likely end of the epoch of the nuclear-tipped intercontinental ballistic missile (ICBM) that has terrified humanity since the first Atlas missile system was declared operational in 1959.

It was the ICBM, especially after the invention of the MIRV warhead (multiple independently targeted reentry vehicle) that destabilized Mutual Assured Destruction (MAD). MAD perpetuated the deterrent effect of the nuclear weapons originated by the Manhattan Project under Robert Oppenheimer and General Leslie Groves. Celebrated in the prize-winning film *Oppenheimer*, this renowned venture mobilized Jews who had fled to the United States from the Holocaust to win World War II for the West. Hugely magnifying the difficulty of thwarting the nuclear threat, MIRVs raised the possibility that either America or the Soviets might be able to launch a successful nuclear first strike against the other by destroying the enemy's nuclear arsenal on the ground.

Unlike an anti-MIRV treaty such as the Strategic Arms Limitation Treaty of 2011 (that rewards violators with surprise), Israel is actually neutralizing the threat. The whole world by now knows of Iron Dome, the Israeli anti-missile system that has been routinely shooting down short-range rockets launched against it from Gaza and Lebanon since it first became operational in 2011. But Iron Dome was merely the first step on a learning curve leading to systems that today are downing mid-to-long-range ballistic missiles while still in the space portion of their flight.

The Iron Dome itself is widely disparaged by Israel's critics as a primitive tool effective only against "homemade" rockets fired by under-funded guerillas. To the contrary, even on the day it was launched, the Iron Dome was the most advanced defense system ever deployed against short-range ballistic missiles. Complaints that the system is "only 90 percent effective" miss the fact that no other air defense has ever approached that standard.

Reports that Iron Dome was overwhelmed by the massive missile barrage from Hamas on October 7, 2023, are mostly jihadist propaganda. Opposing some 2,500 incoming missiles (Hamas propaganda claims there were 5,000) was bound to produce a less than 90 percent success rate. Nevertheless, as a result of artificial intelligence tools that enabled the system to focus only on accurately targeted warheads, damage from the attacks was remarkably light.

So sophisticated is the system that the US, despairing of achieving something as good under an American weapons development system smothered in bureaucracy and "oversight," long ago made the Israelis a deal. America would largely fund the actual missiles if Israel would share the intellectual property of the system. Now Iron Dome's successor projects promise to liberate the world from the threat of long-range ballistic missiles. "David's Sling," operational since 2017, is designed to shoot down medium-range ballistic missiles and rockets with ranges up to 190 miles.

Developed in response the disappointing performance of the American Patriot missiles against Iraqi Scuds during the first Gulf War, David's Sling has proved itself repeatedly in combat. In May 2023 it downed two Iranian made Badr-3 rockets (with a claimed range of approximately 100 miles) launched from Gaza. During the 2024 conflict, it has downed at least one Ayyash-250 rocket with a claimed range of 155 miles. For David's Sling, as with the Iron Dome, Israel supplied the brains via its Rafael development group, while the US put up the money for Raytheon to manufacture the weapons.

Even more impressive yet is the Arrow system designed to intercept much longer-range missiles during space-flight. A regional-range and potential ICBM killer, the program originated from Israel's decision to participate in the Strategic Defense Initiative launched by President Reagan. In the United States, SDI long made only pitiful progress, snarled by political opposition, committee meetings galore, and outright ridicule at Ronald Reagan's idea of "hitting a bullet with a bullet."

That's just what Arrow does.

On October 31, 2023, the Arrow-2 system intercepted a missile incoming from the Red Sea off Yemen (presumably fired by the Houthis) at an altitude of sixty miles. That's well above the stratosphere and the mesosphere at the edge of true outer space, making the encounter the first space combat in human history. Just over a week later, on November 9, 2023, the even more capable Arrow-3 system downed another ballistic missile from Yemen targeting the port city of Eilat, with its population of 52,000, a distance of more than 1,000 miles.

Arrow, like Iron Dome and David's Sling, is a product of the combination of Israeli technological genius and US dollars, with Boeing the American partner. According to senior US Missile Defense Agency officials, this scheme "will be more capable than anything the US even has on its drawing board."

Israel's contribution goes well beyond her engineering prowess. The US could have blazed this trail, as President Reagan wanted us to do. Israel's greatest gift to us, under the pressure of necessity, was that it did not give up. Now that Israel has embarrassed the American and European defense establishments by doing what both had proclaimed was impossible, we may expect the laggards to catch up and start doing their part. Without Israel's example they would not even be in the game.

Ultimately, laser weapons will replace hitting bullets with bullets. Lasers propagating at the speed of light, rapid-firing multiple "rounds" each costing not tens of thousands but a few dollars' worth of electricity will do to missiles (and all aircraft) what the machine gun did to the cavalry charge. After several decades of agonizingly slow development, in just the past couple of years the United States, the United Kingdom, China, and Russia have all demonstrated truly impressive missile-destroying laser weapons.

Once again, however, Israel that may get there first for the same reason that it was the first to hit a bullet with a bullet.

Under constant existential threat, Israel brings new weapons to the field faster than any other country. This is in part because it is willing to learn on the job, introducing novel weapons while other defense establishments are still critiquing, still meeting in committees, still making the perfect the enemy of the good.

Already deployed is Israel's "Iron Beam," a relatively short-range laser weapon that will supplement Iron Dome. Today, still with relatively low power, the Iron Beam takes several seconds to destroy durable targets, allowing many to escape its impact. Iron Beam's great advantage, however, is the low cost of each shot. No one wants to waste a $20,000 Iron Dome missile on a $200 drone.

With Iron Beam operational, and its several times more powerful successor already in development (Lockheed Martin is the American partner), Israel is already on the learning curve. My prediction is that the IDF will have true laser weapons capable of destroying regional or intercontinental missiles before any other western power.

Recognizing and acknowledging the contributions of Israelis to the global economy and to the defense of the West constitutes an Israel Test for all of us. The outsized contributions of Jews to America and the world, however, raise the question of the lost contributions of all the Jews murdered in the Holocaust and in previous and subsequent pogroms. They were killed by people who responded to excellence and achievement with envy, genocidal anger, and hatred rather than with admiration and emulation.

In 2009, Professor Sergio Della Pergola, an Italian-Israeli demographer and statistician, estimated that in 1940 there were eight Jews for every thousand people in the world. Today there are two per thousand. This means that but for the Holocaust there would be some thirty-two million Jews worldwide today rather than the current thirteen million. The eminent columnist, George Will, has made an analogous estimate that if Jews retained their share of world population at the time of Christ, they would number some 200 million today.

The losses for all of us are incalculable. The Israel Test continues. There is no more important test for Americans.

The message of *The Israel Test* can be summed up: Don't worry America, as long as Israel remains behind you.

George Gilder
Huaysompoi, Changmai, Thailand
13 February, 2024

CHAPTER ONE

THE CENTRAL ISSUE

A central issue in international politics, dividing the world into two fractious armies, is the tiny State of Israel.

This central issue is not a global war of civilizations between the West and Islam or a split between Arabs and Jews. These conflicts are real and salient, but they obscure a deeper moral and ideological war. The real issue is between the rule of law and the rule of the leveler, between creative excellence and "fairness," between admiration of achievement versus envy and resentment of it.

Israel represents a line of demarcation. On one side, marshaled at the United Nations and in universities around the globe, are those who see capitalism as a zero-sum game in which success comes at the expense of the poor and the environment: every gain for one party comes at the cost of another. On the other side are those who see the genius and the good fortune of some as a source of wealth and opportunity for all.

The test will lead you to several key questions: What is your attitude toward people who surpass you in the creation of wealth or in other accomplishments? Do you aspire to equal their excellence, or does it make you seethe with rage? Do you admire and celebrate exceptional achievement, or do you impugn it and seek to tear it down? Caroline Glick, the dauntless Israeli author and journalist, has summed it up: "Some people admire success; some people envy it. The enviers hate Israel."

The Israel Test is a moral challenge. The world has learned to see moral challenges as issues of charity and compassion toward victims, especially the poor, whose poverty is seen as proof of their victimization. But the moral challenge of this century is not charity toward the poor but treatment of the productive elites who create the wealth that supports us all. A victim of global resentment, Israel epitomizes the plight of the productive elites under siege around the globe.

In countries where Jews are free to invent and create, they amass conspicuous wealth that arouses envy and suspicion. In this information age, when achievements of the mind have widely outpaced the power of the masses and material force, Jews have forged much of the science and wealth of the era. Their pioneering contributions to quantum theory enabled the digital age. Their breakthroughs in nuclear science and computer science propelled the West to victory in World War II and the Cold War. Their bioengineering inventions have enhanced the health, and their microchip designs are fueling the growth, of nations everywhere. Their genius has lifted the culture and economy of the world.

Israel today concentrates the genius of the Jews. Obscured by the prevalent media narrative of the "war-torn" Middle East, Israel's rarely-celebrated feats of commercial, scientific, and technological creativity are a living testament to the Jews' twentieth-century saga of triumph over tragedy. Today tiny Israel, with its population of 9.6 million, of which 7.1 million are Jewish, is second only to the United States in technological contributions. In per capita innovation, Israel dwarfs all nations. The forces of civilization in the world continue to feed upon the intellectual wealth epitomized by Israel.

Today in the Middle East, Israeli wealth looms palpably and portentously over the middens of Arab poverty. But dwarfing Israel's own wealth is Israel's contribution to the world economy, stemming from Israeli creativity and entrepreneurial innovation. Israel's technical and scientific gifts to global progress loom with similar majesty over all others' contributions with the sole exception of the United States.

Long before the founding of Israel in 1948, Jewish pioneers in Palestine had reclaimed the land from malarial marshes, gullied hillsides, and sand dunes, and enabled it—for the first time in a millennium—to sustain a population of millions of Jews and Arabs alike. Now, over the last three decades, Israel has unleashed a miracle of creative capitalism and technology and exported its contributions around the globe. During the 1990s and early 2000s Israel removed the manacles of its confiscatory taxes, oppressive regulations, government ownership, and socialist nostalgia to establish itself as a driving force of global technological leadership.

Contemplating this Israeli achievement, the minds of parochial intellects around the globe, from Jerusalem to Los Angeles, are clouded with envy and suspicion. Everywhere, from the cagey diplomats of the United Nations to the cerebral leftists at the Harvard Faculty Club, critics of Israel assert that the Jews of Israel are somehow responsible for Palestinian Arab poverty. Violence against Israel is seen as blowback from previous crimes of the Israelis. With little or no extenuation for the difficulties of a targeted defense against the depredations of Hamas burning Jewish babies, raping Jewish girls and women, barbarously killing Jews in horrifying ways, not to mention the decades of guerrilla attacks, suicide bombers, rockets and missiles, the world condemns the Israelis' efforts to preserve and defend their country against those who would destroy it. Denying to Israel the basic rights enjoyed by other nations around the world, as well as the moral fruits and affirmations that Jews have so richly earned by their paramount contributions to our civilization, the critics of Israel lash out at the foundations of civilization itself—at the golden rule of capitalism, that the good fortune of others is also one's own.

In simplest terms, amid the festering indigence and seething violence of the Middle East, the State of Israel presents a test. Efflorescent in the desert, militarily powerful, industrially preeminent, culturally cornucopian, technologically paramount, it has become a vanguard of human achievement. Believing that this position was somehow maliciously captured, rather than heroically created, many in the West still manifest a dangerous misunderstanding of both economics and life.

Assuming that wealth is distributed from above, chiefly by government, rather than generated by the invention and ingenuity of gifted individuals, Israel's critics see the world as a finite sum of resources. They regard economic life as a potentially violent struggle of each against all for one's "fair share." Believing that Israel, like the United States, has seized too much of the world's resources, they advocate vast programs of international retribution and redistribution. They imagine that the plight of the Palestinians reflects not their own Marxist angst, anti-Semitic obsessions, and recidivist violence but the actions of Israel. In their view, Israel's wealth stems not from Jewish creativity and genius but from cadging aid from the United States or seizing valuable land and other resources from Arabs.

In the blinkered view of economists and politicians in both international organizations and elite universities, this tiny bustling country—confined to a space smaller than New Jersey—is a continuation of the history of Western colonialism and imperialism. It is as if an embattled span of a few miracle miles in the desert echoes in some way a map of the world bathed in British pink or Soviet gray. In an elaborately mounted argument, full of pedantic references to Algeria and other colonial wars, Rafael Reuveny, a former Israeli army officer, now an Indiana University professor, declares that Israel is "The Last Colonialist." From the fruited plains of America, he actually finds it possible to write of Israel's "vast lands."

The irony is that Israel is an imperial influence. Its hegemony stems not from its territorial aspirations or desperate efforts to contrive a defensible country amid compulsively predatory neighbors but from the global sway of its ideas and technologies.

To mistake the globally enriching gifts of spirit and intellect for the brutal exercise of force is the central lie of Marxist economics. Although

Karl Marx sometimes affirmed the role of the bourgeoisie in creating wealth, he believed that the entrepreneurial contribution was transitory. The crude Marxian deceit was to declare that all value ultimately derives from labor and materials. Denying the necessary role of the creative mind as expressed in capital and technology, Marx ended up vindicating the zero-sum vision of anti-Semitic envy, in which bankers, capitalists, arbitrageurs, shopkeepers, entrepreneurs, and traders are deemed to be parasitical shysters and dispensable middlemen.

As one of the world's most profitable economies built on one of the world's most barren territories, Israel challenges all these materialist superstitions of zero-sum economics, based on the "distribution" of natural resources and the exploitation of land and labor.

This crippling error of zero-sum economics manifests itself around the globe. It is still the chief cause of poverty. It can destroy any national economy. Perhaps some readers share it. You may believe that capitalist achievement comes at the expense of others or of the environment. You may believe that "behind every great fortune is a great crime." You advocate the redistribution of wealth. You think we all benefit when the government "spreads the wealth around." You imagine that free international trade is a mixed blessing, with many victims. You want to give much of Israel's wealth to its neighbors. You think that Israel's neighbors—and the world—would benefit more from redistribution than from Israel's continuing prosperity and freedom. You believe that Israel is somehow too large rather than too small. You believe, fantastically, that poverty is caused by enterprise and the ownership of private property—that poverty is, ineluctably, a grievous side effect of wealth.

Anti-Semites throughout history have been obsessed with the "gaps" everywhere discernible between different groups: gaps of income, power, achievement, and status. Against the background of Arab poverty, anti-capitalists and anti-Semites alike see Israel as primarily a creator not of wealth but of gaps. With a gross domestic product of around $488.5 billion (2021), per capita income of some $52,100, (2021) and $1,008,956,800 of market capitalization for its companies, Israel these days is rich, they say. But look at the gap between its luxuries and Palestinian privation. Look at the gap between Jews in Israel and Arabs in Israel—sure evidence of "discrimination" and "exploitation." Similarly, Jews lead all other American groups in per capita income, signifying another gap, presumably rectifiable by the United Nations.

Shaping the clichés of the gapologists is a profound misunderstanding. What makes capitalism succeed is not chiefly its structure of incentives but its use of knowledge and experience. As a system of accumulated knowledge, capitalism assigns to the entrepreneurs who have already proven their prowess as investors—who have moved down the learning curve in the investment process—the right to shape the future pattern of investments. The lessons of one generation of successful investments inform the next generation. The lessons of failure are learned rather than submerged in subsidies and gilded with claims of higher virtue and purpose. Information is accumulated rather than lost. Under capitalism, knowledge increases apace with wealth.

Disguising this edifying process in the United States are the handicapitalists in nominally "private" institutions—from Wall Street money-shufflers and government-guaranteed mortgage hustlers to corn-state ethanol farmers and Silicon Valley solar shills—that are dependent on public handouts and mandates for their success. As explained in definitive works by the Israeli economist Daniel Doron and by the writer Jonah Goldberg in the United States, a perpetual temptation of democratic politics in Israel, the US, and in other countries around the globe is the use of government to reward political supporters, creating government-corporate alliances that are fascist rather than capitalist in character. In successful economies these alliances remain marginal, rather than central as they are in explicitly socialist regimes.

If governments were superior investors, the Soviet bloc would have been an economic triumph rather than an economic and environmental catastrophe. China would have thrived under Mao rather than under the current regime that claims, "To get rich is glorious." Whether in the United States or in Israel, at Harvard or at the United Nations, an obsessive concern with gaps between rich and poor is the hallmark of a deep and persistent Marxism that is intrinsically hostile to the wealth-producing work of Jews in the world. At the heart of the UN's case against Israel is the UN's maniacal focus on gaps.

Misunderstanding the nature of capitalism, the critics turn to challenge Israeli democracy. They charge that Israel's Jewish identity creates serious problems for its democratic values. Like former president Jimmy Carter in his book *Palestine: Peace Not Apartheid*, former Israeli foreign minister Shlomo Ben-Ami in an article in *Foreign Affairs*, the flamboyant Frenchman Bernard-Henri Lévy in articles and a book, *Left in Dark Times*, and Thomas L. Friedman in a series of books and in his *New York Times* columns, many people raise the chimera of a Jewish "apartheid" regime that will mar the purity of Israel as a homeland for Jews.

The apartheid claim is based on the possibility that at some future date Arab Palestinians will comprise a majority of the population under Israeli control. But Jews in Israel are already a minority in the region and will always be a minority. Once the Arab nations learn to tolerate the existence of the Jewish state, some federal system involving Jordan would be the next step for any Palestinian nationalism that transcends a mere desire to destroy Israel. Equating democracy not with the rule of law but with the claims of racist self-determination, even nominally pro-Israel writers imply that nine million Jews are morally obliged to entrust their fate to some 100 million Arabs pledged to banish Israel from the region if not from the world.

This bizarre conclusion is the perfectly logical result of the fondest dream of the twentieth-century Left, to reconcile democracy and socialism, to imagine democracy without economic freedom or a system of law and property rights that transcend the vicissitudes of elections. Democracy without capitalism has no content, since no power-centers outside the state can form and sustain themselves. As a form of politics, dealing with relative power, democracy by itself is a zero-sum game, in which the winnings of one group come at the cost of others. There are only a limited number of seats in a legislature or executive positions in a government, only a limited span of territory to rule. By contrast, capitalism is a positive-sum game, based on an upward spiral of gains, with no limits to the creation of wealth. Under capitalism, the achievements of one group provide markets and opportunities for all. Without an expanding capitalist economy, democracy becomes dominated by its zero-sum elements—by mobs and demagogues.

Throughout history, in every nation with a significant Jewish population, such mobs and demagogues have turned against the Jews. Today they have turned against Israel. And Jimmy Carter, Thomas Friedman, and all the rest who advocate the claims of Arab "democracy" over Israeli accomplishment unintentionally side with the mobs and demagogues. Their equation of democracy with ethnic self-determination transforms democracy into a figment of tribal polling rather than a defensible polity. It puts Israel into a queue of petitioners with such entities as Tibet or Burma, Kosovo or Bosnia as if these were comparable to Israel.

Non-capitalist self-determination, though, is entirely self-defeating. Sleek new automobiles across the United States—Priuses and Teslas galore—bear bumper stickers declaring, "Co-Exist," "War is Not the Answer" or urging a "Free Tibet," as if Tibet could be freed with hortatory vehicular adornments. Without capitalism and free trade, self-determination is a pretext for constant civil wars, as each ever-smaller shard of nationality seeks its own exclusive domain, presumably to be defended by the United States or the United Nations.

The critical test of democracy is its ability to free human energies and intellect on the frontiers of human accomplishment. More than any other country in the world, Israel resplendently passes this test. It is the test of *zerizus*, Hebrew for "alacrity," or, as Rabbi Zelig Pliskin describes it on the *Jewish World Review* website, "the blessed willpower and aspiration that leads to exceptional achievement." Passing this test, Israel is precious. All the carping and criticisms of Israel reflect a blind proceduralism and empty egalitarianism. The test of virtue is not mere procedure; it exemplifies content and accomplishment. If a system cannot pass this test—democratic or not, concerned with electoral politics or not—it is just another form of barbarism.

In his masterpiece, *The Revolt of the Masses*, José Ortega y Gasset described the essential barbarian mentality as a failure or refusal to recognize our dependence on the exceptional men and women who created the civilization in which we live and on which we subsist. Like monkeys in the jungle reaching for low-hanging fruit without any clue of its source or science, the barbarian politicians leading the ranks of modern anti-Semitism promiscuously pick the fruits of modern capitalism and the pockets of capitalists without a clue as to the provenance of their own largely parasitical lives and luxuries.

More sharply and categorically than any other conflict, the Israel-Palestine dispute raises these issues of capitalism and democracy, civilization and barbarism. To many observers—in the army of the Left—it is obvious that Israeli wealth causes Palestinian misery. How could it be otherwise? Jews have long been paragons of capitalist wealth. Capitalist wealth, as Pierre-Joseph Proudhon, the nineteenth century French socialist and economist, put it in regard to "property," is "theft." Marx was said to have shaped his opposition to property rights and his own Jewish self-hatred by reading the even more virulently anti-Semitic Proudhon. In an 1883 diary entry, Proudhon wrote, "The Jew is the enemy of mankind. One must send this race back to Asia or be exterminated."

History, however, favors the view that poverty springs chiefly from envy and hatred of excellence—from class-war Marxism, anti-Semitism, and kleptocratic madness. It stems from the belief that wealth inheres in things and material resources that can be seized and redistributed, rather than in human minds and creations that thrive only in peace and freedom. In particular, the immiseration of the Middle East stems from the covetous and crippling idea among Arabs that Israel's wealth is not only the source of their humiliation but also the cause of their poverty and thus an appropriate target of their vengeance.

This is the most portentous form of the Israel test. Inescapably, it poses the questions of life and wealth that lie behind nearly all the holocausts and massacres of recent world history, from the genocidal attacks on European Jews and the pogroms of Russian Kulaks and Jews to Maoist China's murderous "cultural revolution," from the eviction of white settlers and Indian entrepreneurs from Africa to the massacres of overseas Chinese businessmen in Indonesia. The pattern recurs in the pillage and murders of "privileged" Kikuyu shopkeepers and "wealthy" Rift Valley long-distance runners after the 2007 Kenyan elections.

Everywhere, as I wrote in *Wealth & Poverty*, the horrors and the bodies pile up, in the world's perennial struggle to rid itself of the menace of riches—of the shopkeepers, the bankers, the merchants, the *middlemen*, the traders, the landowning farmers, the entrepreneurs—"at the same time that the toll also mounts in victims of unnecessary famine and poverty. Everywhere nations claim a resolve to *develop*; but everywhere their first goal is to expropriate, banish, or kill the very people doing the developing. At the United Nations, these contradictions reach a polyglot climax, with alternating zeal against the blight of want and against the Americans and Zionists, the creators of wealth."

With wealth seen as stolen from the exploited poor, the poor are, in turn, granted a license to dispossess and kill their "oppressors" and to disrupt capitalist economies. This is the message of Frantz Fanon, Hamas, al-Qaida, Hezbollah, and the academic coteries of Noam Chomsky, Howard Zinn, and a thousand Marxist myrmidons across the campuses of the world. But no capitalist system can sustain prosperity amid constant violence, spurred by the idea that suicide bombing is an understandable and forgivable response to alleged gaps and grievances.

It is the violence that makes necessary the police measures that render economic progress impossible, particularly for the groups associated with the attacks. By justifying violent assaults on a civilized democracy—and then condemning the necessary retaliatory defense—leftists would allow no solution but tyranny, with Jewish minorities widely under attack and the sole Jewish state in jeopardy.

Most of the world's experts—advocates and critics of Israel alike—are blind to the Israel test. G. K. Chesterton got it right. "The Fabian argument of the expert, that the man who is trained should be the man who is trusted, would be absolutely unanswerable if it were really true that a man who studied a thing and practiced it every day went on seeing more and more of its significance. But he does not. He goes on seeing less and less of its significance."

From the virtuoso tracts of Alan Dershowitz to the demented screeds of Chomsky or Naomi Klein, from the casuistic pirouettes of Michael Lerner and his *Tikkun* magazine to the pro-Israel celebrations of the Religious Right, from Jeffrey Goldberg in the *Atlantic* to Bernard-Henri Lévy, the literature of Israeli condemnation and support—however coherent on its own terms—seems mostly irrelevant to the real test and trial of Israel.

Beyond the wholehearted endorsements of the Religious Right—including the ten million-member Christians United For Israel—which are unlikely to convince anyone else, the general position of the experts is that Israel is deeply flawed but commands a colorable case for continued existence. Coloring the case entails much knowledge of the intricacies of international law and the history of UN resolutions. Israel's historical record is said to be full of excessive violence, but it is extenuated by the violence inflicted on the Jews in the Holocaust. These self-appointed experts argue that Israel may not be good, but it has rights that should be respected, provided that it improves its behavior.

By clinging to liberal policy and democratic processes, Israel, in this view, may justify its claim to continued American aid. Under these conditions, says even the Third Worldly President Barack Obama, the United States should continue to affirm and guarantee the country's defense. Because of Israel's legal rights and democratic processes, the United States should ignore the country's dire unpopularity with nearly all of its allies, international organizations, and trading partners that condemn its allegedly lawless and aggressive foreign policy.

At their best, these defenders of Israel pile up impressive mountains of evidence that Israel is "not guilty" of charges only a madman, a delusional academic, or a UN human rights expert could have brought in the first place. Alan Dershowitz, the distinguished *emeritus* law professor at Harvard, has written, as of 2024, a total of eleven popular books, including *The Case for Israel* and *The Case Against Israel's Enemies*, that offer dozens of chapters with powerful evidence against the standard propaganda. He is among the best and most tenacious defenders Israel has, outside of the incandescent pages of *Commentary*, and he has millions more readers than that remarkable publication.

Not for nothing is Dershowitz one of the world's leading defense attorneys. But the very act of responding to the claims of diabolical maniacs puts this great advocate of Israel in an inappropriately defensive posture, as if a country that requires so resourceful, agile, and punctilious a defense—like one of Dershowitz's most notable former clients, Claus von Bulow—must have something to hide, a skeleton in its Knesset, a metastasized horror in its history.

The central error of Israel's defenders is to accept the framing of the debate by its enemies, whose idea is that peace depends on some marginal but perpetually elusive improvement in Israel's behavior. Prefacing the usual defense are concessions that Israel is "far from perfect" and "has made mistakes" in "overreacting to terrorism and other threats." As former Harvard president Lawrence Summers put it, "There is much…in Israel's foreign and defense policy that can and should be vigorously challenged." Such statements from Israel's nominal defenders slip readily from meaningless negatives: "Israel is not perfect"—to crippling concessions: "Israel overreacts to terror."

Locked in a debate over Israel's alleged vices, they miss the salient truth running through the long history of anti-Semitism: Israel is hated, above all, for its virtues.

No Israeli failure to comply with the dictates of the rulings handed down by the misnamed UN-run International Court of Justice in The Hague defending the free movement of suicide bombers, no Jewish falling short of the standards devised by UN human rights committees dominated by demented tyrants, can even begin to explain, let alone *excuse,* the celebrated kidnappings, burnings, beheadings, and bombings, and the frothy prophecies of extinction and calls to pogroms that reverberate daily through the streets and mosques of the Middle East with the regularity of the muezzin calls to prayer.

From the Palestinian Liberation Organization's (PLO) 1964 announcement, long before Israel had control of the West Bank or Gaza, of its resolve to extinguish the State of Israel by "armed struggle," to the daily calls by the venerable president of Egypt Gamal Abdel Nasser for "Israel's destruction" in the 1967 war; from the prime minister of Syria, Haffez al-Assad, invoking "a battle of annihilation," to two recent presidents of Iran pledging to "wipe Israel off the map"; from the endless proclamations by Palestinian terrorist politicians and American college students seeking "liberation from the Jordan River to the sea," to the various men of Allah declaring that Jews are "filthy bacteria" that must be "butchered and killed...wherever you meet them"; from the sponsorship and celebration of suicide bombers by various imams and exalted rulers, to polls of the Palestinian people affirming the same murderous worldview; these statements are no frenzied war cries uttered only during actual combat and regretted in peacetime. Representing the essence of the Palestinian movement, rabid anti-Semitism continues a commitment that began with Palestinian complicity in the Holocaust.

Everyone knows that the word "Nazi" is used promiscuously in today's world. But the word does have a real meaning. It means the National Socialist Movement dedicated to murderous anti-Semitism. Socialism everywhere expresses envy of excellence by treating the works and wealth of the successful as the wages of sin. Nazism simply specifies the sin as the result of a Jewish conspiracy.

By this definition, the PLO has always been, at its essence, a Nazi organization. The first move toward pushing the Jews into the sea came during World War II from the Grand Mufti of Jerusalem, Haj Amin al-Husseini. "Germany," as the Mufti put it, "is the only country in the world that has not merely fought the Jews at home but has declared war on the entirety of world Jewry; in this war against world Jewry the Arabs feel profoundly connected to Germany."

Fresh from aiding the massacre of Jews in Romania and Bosnia and recruiting Bosnian Muslims into the Nazi forces, the Mufti was a fanatical participant in the European Holocaust. His most passionate goal was to extend it to the Middle East. After visiting Auschwitz with Himmler, this founder-hero of the Palestinian movement urged the Nazis to accelerate and intensify the killings and then join him in extending the carnage to Palestine by massacring the half-million Jews living there. In this pursuit, he conspired with the Nazis under Walther Rauff, engineer of Auschwitz, to create a special force in Greece ready to make the attack. Only the British General Bernard Montgomery's defeat of Rommel at El Alamein prevented the Mufti and his friends from pursuing their plan. Still unsated in his killing frenzies in late 1944, the Grand Mufti launched an attack of parachutists on the Tel Aviv water supply with ten containers of toxin. Failing in the attempt, he devoted the rest of his life to the cause of destroying Israel.

Cited as a war criminal, Husseini gained asylum with the similarly rabid Holocaust celebrants among the Muslim Brotherhood in Egypt. For his barbarities, the Mufti remains a revered historical figure among the Palestinians. Beginning in the 1930s, his Nazi animus originated long before any of the alleged Israeli offenses that are now cited to justify Palestinian violence and hatred against the Jews in Israel.

When Husseini died in 1974, his anti-Semitic cause was taken up by his distant relative Yasser Arafat, the PLO leader and eventual Nobel

"Peace" laureate. Arafat characteristically bought Hitler's *Mein Kampf* in bulk and distributed it to his followers in Arab translation under the title *My Jihad*, as Israeli soldiers discovered on capturing his abandoned camp in southern Lebanon in 1982. Arafat was a master of the duplicitous art of recanting in splenetic Arabic to his followers any public professions of peace he may have expressed in English at international meetings and "summits."

Arafat's successor as head of the Palestinian Authority, Mahmoud Abbas, is supposedly a "moderate." This seems to be the term for anti-Semites who are ambivalent about whether to celebrate the Holocaust or to deny that it occurred. Devoted to the destruction of Israel, Abbas was a Holocaust denier from the time of his doctoral thesis—in his own words, a study of "the Zionist fantasy, the fantastic lie that six million Jews were killed." Contesting Abbas for power and winning Palestinian elections in 2006 was Hamas, an organization whose founding charter proclaims its devotion to the killing of Jews. After Hamas joined Fatah in a unity government in May 2011, Hamas MP and cleric Yunis Al-Astal, declared on Al-Aqsa TV:

All the predators, all the birds of prey, all the dangerous reptiles and insects, and all the lethal bacteria are far less dangerous than the Jews. In just a few years, all the Zionists and the settlers will realize that their arrival in Palestine was for the purpose of the great massacre, by means of which Allah wants to relieve humanity of their evil.

Perhaps the most menacing force for Palestinian "liberation" is Hamas's ally, Hezbollah, whose leader, Hassan Nasrallah, declared in 2002 that if all the Jews gather in Israel, "they'll make our job easier, and will keep us from having to go hunt them down all over the world."

When experts in the United States urge the creation of a Palestinian state, they are effectively endorsing a Nazi national movement with roots in Europe. Pointless and fantastical are claims to favor a Palestinian national movement that renounces the murder of Jews. Murdering Jews is at the heart of the only Palestinian national movement the world has ever known.

The creation of a peaceful and productive Palestinian state would require support from neither Harvard nor Hezbollah, nor any force outside Palestine itself. The Palestinian Arabs could be a nation tomorrow and a state the day after, if their leaders could let go of the notion that the Jews must die before Palestine can live. By merely foreswearing violence and taking advantage of their unique position contiguous with the world's most creative people, the Palestinians could be rich and happy. Civilized people with the good fortune to live near brilliant entrepreneurs or thinkers go to work for them and attempt to learn their skills and master their fields of knowledge. Then they may start similar ventures on their own. It is the only way to succeed. In the past, Palestinian Arabs often excelled as entrepreneurs, and some do so around the world today. But nowhere are the Palestinians less likely to prosper than under the current Palestinian regimes. Palestinian leaders tell their people to disdain the peaceful and collaborative demands of democratic capitalism. Palestinians are taught to say they find it "humiliating" to work for Jews. They are taught that the creation of Israel was their *naqba*, Arabic for a "catastrophe" they believe is comparable to the Holocaust rather than the source of their own nationhood and property. So, like the other self-defeating democrats everywhere in the region, they elect jihadists to drive out the Jews.

In no way do the usual defenders of Israel so clearly concede the National Socialist framing of the debate as on the question of "settlements": the fate of the several hundred thousand Jews living on West Bank territory, land that some Israeli government might concede to a Palestinian state. Dershowitz and scores of other defenders of Israel, including Bernard-Henri Lévy, Thomas Friedman, and Jeffrey Goldberg, join the chorus of critics regarding as a "serious" or even a "catastrophic error" settlements that plant productive people on mostly undeveloped areas of Judea and Samaria that once chiefly sprouted missiles and mortars overlooking Jerusalem and Tel Aviv. Once again, nominal defenders of Israel give up the key point without even seeing it. For the dispute over the settlements is an argument over whether Jews may reasonably expect to be permitted to live among Arabs anywhere.

After the Arabs refused all offers of land for peace in the wake of the 1967 war, the Israelis were necessarily responsible for the West Bank and Gaza. Israel's government under Levi Eshkol initially barred settlements on the grounds that under a peace agreement the land would one day be relinquished to the capacious and underpopulated existing Palestinian state named Jordan. When the Jordanians joined the rest of the Arab states in adamantly refusing any negotiations, Israel inherited the land. Refuting every claim of Arab "displacement" by Jews, the Israelis spurred development and welcomed Arabs thronging in to participate in it. Between the 1967 war and the First Intifada in 1987, Arab settlers, moving in from Jordan and other Arab countries to the West Bank and Gaza, came to outnumber Israeli settlers eight to one.

Since Israel's creation, while it was accommodating massive immigration from Arab nations, essentially every Arab state expelled its own Jews, many resident for generations. Evicted were more than 800,000 people. Confiscated was some $2.5 billion in land and wealth. Rivaling every Nazi dream of ethnic purity are these domains ruled by Arab *sharia* law, anti-Semitism and state socialism.

Every proposal for a Palestinian state, even from Israel's usual supporters, takes this massive crime as a given and proposes that Israel preemptively carry out exactly such an act of "ethnic cleansing" by itself uprooting the Jewish inhabitants from the West Bank. Although Israel accepts both Christians and Muslims as citizens, and indeed includes elected Arab members in its national legislature and in its national army, the Israeli Defense Force, both Israel's enemies and its defenders assume that any future Palestinian state will exclude any remaining Jews from the homes and neighborhoods, communities, shops, and schools they themselves have built. Too bizarre to be contemplated, apparently, is the possibility that the Jews, if they so chose, could be allowed to live in a Palestinian state, or be safe if they did. One of the essential duties of a democratic government is the safeguarding of the rights of its minorities.

At home in the United States, if some locally dominant ethnic group violently protested against Jews being allowed to live on property amounting to 2 percent of "the neighborhood," all these supposed defenders of Israel would know exactly with whom they were dealing and how to respond. But in the case of the Palestinians, we are to accept as their natural right their claims to be squeamish about living anywhere near Jews.

But without the presence of the Jews, there is no evidence that the Palestinians would particularly want these territories for a nation. When they were held under Jordanian and Egyptian rule between 1948 and 1967, after all, there was no significant move to create a Palestinian state, but there was a continuing migration toward the peace and prosperity that the Jews were creating. Hostility toward Jews stems not from any alleged legal violations or untoward violence, but from their exceptional virtues. This is the essence of anti-Semitism.

The Israel test requires a remorseless realism. It disallows all the bumper-sticker contradictions of pacifistic bellicosity. Either the world, principally the United States, supports Israel, or Israel, one way or another, will be destroyed. There are no other realistic choices. And if Israel is destroyed, capitalist Europe will likely die as well, and America, as the protected home of productive and creative capitalism spurred by Jews, will be in jeopardy.

Winston Churchill proclaimed the essential situation in a speech in Parliament in 1939 responding to efforts to withdraw British support for a Jewish state. Describing "the magnificent work which the Jewish colonists have done," he said: "They have made the desert bloom...started a score of thriving industries...founded a great city on the barren shore...harnessed the Jordan and spread its electricity throughout the land....So far from being persecuted, the Arabs have crowded into the country and multiplied till their population has increased more than even all world Jewry could lift up the Jewish population. Now we are asked to decree that all this is to stop and all this is to come to an end. We are now asked to submit—and this is what rankles most with me—to an agitation which is fed with foreign money and ceaselessly inflamed by Nazi and by Fascist propaganda."

That says it all, for the ages. Eighty-five years later nothing much has changed.

CHAPTER TWO

THE TALE OF THE BELL CURVE

The Israel test begins with anti-Semitism, which remains a global plague as persistent and metastatic and multifarious, and as baffling in its etiology, as cancer.

The most compelling book on anti-Semitism that I have encountered is *Why The Jews? The Reason for Antisemitism* by Dennis Prager and Rabbi Joseph Telushkin. I read the first edition when it was published in 1983 and the later edition in 2003. It is lucidly written, intelligent, fervent, and historically sophisticated. It conveys the earnest, wise, and often ironical voice of its Los Angeles-based, talk-radio star co-author, Prager. Although suffused with indignation and a tragic sense of life, it is clear-eyed and dispassionate on the critical issues. What's not to like?

Prager and Telushkin emphasize that anti-Semitism is "unique": it cannot be comprehended as a form of racism, neurosis, antinationalism, envy, ethnic hostility, religious bigotry, or resentment of success. They contend that "modern attempts to dejudaize Jew-hatred, to attribute it to economic, social, and political factors and universalize it into merely another instance of bigotry are as opposed to the facts of Jewish history as they are to the historical Jewish understanding of anti-Semitism."

Prager and Telushkin recount many chilling and telling tales of anti-Semitic horror reaching far back into history, long before the modern forms of Jew-hatred emerged from current economic and political conditions. They also demonstrate that anti-Semitism has reached into

35

the most refined centers of culture and the most learned redoubts of academic intellect—pantheons such as Harvard and the Council on Foreign Relations, despite each having several Jewish presidents, both old haunts of mine—where any other form of racism would be socially leprous and outré. The authors tout the universality of anti-Semitism, its persistence, its protean irrepressibility, its grisly shapes, its ghastly violence, its frequent respectability, its secular animus, and its religious fanaticism as evidence for its monstrous and inexorable uniqueness.

"Anti-Semites have not hated Jews," they write, "because Jews are affluent—poor Jews have always been as hated; or strong—weak Jews have simply invited anti-Semitic bullies; or because Jews may have unpleasant personalities—genocide is not personality generated; or because ruling classes focus worker discontent onto Jews—precapitalist and noncapitalist societies, such as the former Soviet Union, other Communist states, and various third-world countries, have been considerably more anti-Semitic than capitalist societies."

They conclude: "Anti-Semites have hated Jews because Jews are Jewish,"—essentially for the Jewish belief in their chosenness, in their own national identity, and in the universal reach of their monotheistic God and the moral law associated with the God of the Old Testament. Moreover, to salt the wound of anti-Semitic humiliation, practicing Jews enjoy the best revenge. They live well, leading "demonstrably higher-quality lives" than others who do not adhere to Jewish moral and religious tenets. According to Prager and Telushkin, it is these specific characteristics of religious Jews that cause anti-Semitism, rather than the widespread human sins of racism, envy, nationalism, and ethnic hostility that inhere in all other examples of bigotry.

Opening the book is a quotation from the National Conference of Catholic Bishops that sums up the Prager-Telushkin view: "It was Judaism that brought the concept of a God-given universal moral law into the world.... The Jew carries the burden of God in history [and] for this has never been forgiven."

Jewish ethical monotheism and its propagation is a basic gift and goad alike to gentiles and Jews who have accepted a relativist morality and philosophy that condones sexual immorality, abortion, and other convenient forms of hedonism. Ethical monotheism is a cherished contribution to humankind and a resented standard of unattainable righteousness. By evoking faith in the meaning and regularity of the cosmos, it is crucial to Jewish science and business and indeed to all human achievement. As Prager and Telushkin finally contend, it may be the solution to the problem of anti-Semitism. But it is not, as they also argue, its cause.

The world tolerates all sorts and conditions of religious observance, from the Amish to Jehovah's Witnesses, from the Mormons to the Scientologists, and on and on. Many of these faiths include apocalyptic prophecies of the incineration of all their enemies and the survival of a chosen remnant. Some of these faiths evoke scorn, some laughter, most indifference.

Benzion Netanyahu, the late historian father of Israeli Prime Minister Benjamin Netanyahu, has demonstrated in an awesome 500,000-word tome, *The Origins of the Inquisition in Fifteenth-Century Spain,* that the most vicious anti-Jewish acts of mass destruction and devastation not only preceded the emergence of Christianity but also represented a reaction against the *secular* power achieved by Jews. He vividly describes the ineffably horrific persecution in Alexandria that was conducted by Hellenistic Egyptians in 38 AD. It was described contemporaneously by the Jewish historian Philo of Alexandria thusly: "the most merciless of all their persecutors in some instances burnt whole families, husbands with their wives, and infant children with their parents, in the middle of the city, sparing neither age nor youth, nor the innocent helplessness of infants." Some men, he says, were dragged to death, while "those who did these things, mimicked the sufferers, like people employed in the representation of theatrical farces." Other Jews were crucified. Netanyahu concludes: "We agree with that clear-sighted scholar who said,

unreservedly, in plain language: 'Anti-Semitism was born in Egypt.'"
His book shows that motivating the Inquisition in Spain was not hostility to Jewish religion but rage against the superior effectiveness and
ascendancy of Jews outperforming established clerics as *Christians.*
"New Christians," mostly Jewish, were taking over the Spanish church
by being more learned, eloquent, devout, resourceful, and charismatic
than Christian leaders. As Netanyahu writes, "The struggle against the
Jews was essentially motivated by social and economic, rather than
religious considerations."

For all their sage observations, Prager and Telushkin miss the heart
of the matter, which is the fact of Jewish intellectual and entrepreneurial
superiority. As the eminent philosemitic Russian writer, Maxim Gorky,
put it: "Whatever nonsense the anti-Semites may talk, they dislike the
Jew only because he is obviously better, more adroit, and more capable of
work than they are." Whether driven by culture or genes—or, like most
behavior, an inextricable mix—the fact of Jewish genius is demonstrable.
It can be gainsaid only by people who cannot expect to be believed. The
source of anti-Semitism is Jewish superiority and excellence.

The entire debate over Israel currently rides on a tacit subtext of crucial matters too sensitive to be probed, such as the central contributions
of Jews to global science, technology, art, and prosperity; proprieties that
cannot be transgressed, such as pointing to the comparative brutality
and barrenness of its adversaries; and immense realities that cannot be
broached, such as the manifest supremacy of Jews over all other ethnic
groups in nearly every intellectual, commercial, and cultural endeavor.

In *The Bell Curve,* Charles Murray and Richard Herrnstein pointed
to the massive superiority in IQs of Ashkenazi (Eastern European) Jews
over all other genetically identifiable groups. The outlying region of the
curve is massively Jewish.

As Murray later distilled the evidence in *Commentary,* the Jewish
mean intelligence quotient is 110, ten points over the norm. This strik-
ingly higher average intelligence, however, is not the decisive factor in

overall Jewish achievement. As recently as 1999, Israelis of all ethnicities failed *on average* to outperform Americans in international tests of eighth-grade math and science skills. In math, Israelis ranked just behind Thailand and Moldova and one place ahead of Tunisia. Israel lagged nine places behind the United States, whose performance is usually deemed miserably far behind the leading Asian and European performers. In science, the numbers were similar.

What matters in human accomplishment is not the average performance but the treatment of exceptional performance and the cultivation of genius. The commanding lesson of Jewish accomplishment is that genius trumps everything else. As Murray and Herrnstein write, "The key indicator for predicting *exceptional* accomplishment (like winning a Nobel Prize) is the incidence of exceptional intelligence....The proportion of Jews with IQs of 140 or higher is somewhere around six times the proportion of everyone else." This proportion rises at still higher IQs. Murray and Herrnstein report a study made in 1954 of IQs in the New York public school system that showed Jews with some 85 percent of the IQs over 170 (twenty-four out of twenty-eight). This superiority in IQ also expressed itself in excellence in games that demand exceptional intelligence. Since the 1880s, nearly half of all the world chess champions have been of Jewish heritage.

Such stunning findings in *The Bell Curve* aroused little comment. Critics focused instead on a few provocative lines on the possible influence of genetic endowment in the IQs of blacks, although the margin of Jewish superiority over other whites was at least as large as the white edge over blacks and less amenable to sociological extenuation.

This reaction is typical of the great error of contemporary social thought: that poverty results not from the behavior or lesser capabilities of the poor, or the corruptions of failed cultures, but from "discrimination." In the current era, Jews will always tend to be overrepresented at the pinnacles of intellectual excellence. Therefore an ideological belief that nature favors equal outcomes fosters hostility to capitalism and leads directly and inexorably to anti-Semitism. These egalitarian attitudes are the chief source of poverty in the world.

Poverty needs no explanation. It has been the usual condition of nearly all human beings throughout history. When poverty occurs in modern capitalist societies it is invariably a result of cultural collapse, typified by the American ghetto or Gaza or the West Bank or southern Lebanon, because young men are deprived of productive models of masculinity. What is precious and in need of explanation and nurture is the special configuration of cultural and intellectual aptitudes and practices—the differences, the inequalities—that under some rare and miraculous conditions have produced wealth for the world. Inequality is the answer, not the problem.

Murray's later work, *Human Accomplishment*, focused on the fact that, as judged by Murray's complex calculus fed by a database of historians, the Jewish three-tenths of one percent of the entire population of the world has contributed some 25 percent of recent notable intellectual accomplishment in the modern period. Murray cites the historical record: "In the first half of the twentieth century, despite pervasive and continuing social discrimination against Jews throughout the Western world, despite the retraction of legal rights, and despite the Holocaust, Jews won 14 percent of Nobel Prizes in literature, chemistry, physics, and medicine/physiology." He then proceeds to more recent data: "In the second half of the twentieth century, when Nobel Prizes began to be awarded to people from all over the world, that figure [of Jews awarded Nobel Prizes] rose to 29 percent. So far in the twenty-first century, it has been 32 percent."

From the day Heinrich Hertz, whose father was a Jew, first demonstrated electromagnetic waves and Albert Michelson conducted the key experiments underlying Einstein's theory of relativity, the achievements of modern science are largely the expression of Jewish genius and ingenuity. If 26 percent of Nobel Prizes do not suffice to make the case, it is confirmed by 51 percent of the Wolf Foundation Prizes in

Physics, 28 percent of the Max Planck Medailles and 38 percent of the Dirac Medals for Theoretical Physics, 37 percent of the Heineman Prizes for Mathematical Physics, and 53 percent of the Enrico Fermi Awards.

Jews are not only superior in abstruse intellectual pursuits, such as quantum physics and nuclear science. They are also heavily over-represented among entrepreneurs of the technological businesses that lead and expand the global economy. Social psychologist David McClelland, author of *The Achieving Society*, found that entrepre-neurs are identified by a greater "need for achievement" than are other groups. There is little doubt, he concludes, explaining the dis-proportionate representation of Jews among entrepreneurs, that in the United States the average need for achievement is higher among Jews than in the general population.

"Need for achievement" alone, however, will not enable a person to start and run a successful technological company. That takes a combina-tion of technological mastery, business prowess, and leadership skills that is not evenly distributed even among elite scientists and engineers. Edward B. Roberts of the Massachusetts Institute of Technology's Sloan School of Management compared MIT graduates who launched new technological companies with a control group of graduates who pursued other careers. The largest factor in predicting an entrepreneurial career in technology was an entrepreneurial father. Controlling for this factor, he discovered that Jews were *five times* more likely to start technological enterprises than other MIT graduates.

These remarkable facts and their powerful implications have evoked surprisingly little discussion. But a book such as Prager and Telushkin's *Why the Jews?* on anti-Semitism that fails to come to terms with the raw facts of Jewish intellectual superiority will fail to persuade its readers, who will sense that the argument cannot bear the weight it is asked to carry. Yes, there is a religious component in anti-Semitism, but there is also a political and economic element, reflected in the objective anti-Semitism of Marx, Chomsky, Friedrich Engels, Zinn, Naomi Klein, and other Jewish leftists who above all abhor capitalism. Jews, amazingly, excel so readily in all intellectual fields that they outperform all rivals even in the arena of anti-Semitism.

For all its special features and extreme manifestations, anti-Semitism is a reflection of the hatred toward successful middlemen, entrepreneurs, shopkeepers, lenders, bankers, financiers, and other capitalists that is visible everywhere whenever an identifiable set of outsiders outperforms the rest of the population in the economy. This is true whether the offending excellence comes from the Kikuyu in Kenya, the Ibo and the Yoruba in Nigeria, the overseas Indians and whites in Uganda and Zimbabwe, the Lebanese in West Africa, South America, and around the world, the Parsis in India, the Indian Gujaratis in South and East Africa, the Armenians in the Ottoman Empire, and above all—the more than thirty million overseas Chinese in Indonesia, Malaysia, and elsewhere in Southeast Asia.

Thomas Sowell of the Hoover Institution reports that in Indonesia overseas Chinese constituted only five percent of the population, but they controlled 70 percent of private domestic capital and ran three-quarters of the nation's top 200 businesses. Their economic dominance—and their repeated victimization in ghastly massacres—prompts Sowell to comment: "Although the overseas Chinese have long been known as the 'Jews of Southeast Asia,' perhaps Jews might more aptly be called the overseas Chinese of Europe."

Sowell has written several books that document this pattern of hostility toward "middleman minorities" in fascinating detail and has explained its causes and effects with convincing authority. The role of wealth creation and trade, with its rigorous disciplines, linguistic virtuosity, and accounting prowess, means that "middleman minorities must be very different from their customers." These groups, "their wealth inexplicable, their superiority intolerable," typically arouse hatred from competing intellectuals. "It is not usually the masses of the people who most resent the more productive people in their midst. More commonly, it is the intelligentsia, who may with sufficiently sustained effort spread their own resentments to others."

The culture of economic advance "and the social withdrawal needed to preserve this differentness in their children," Sowell writes, "leave the middleman minorities vulnerable to charges of 'clannishness' by political and other demagogues.... These accusations can exploit racial, religious, or other differences, but this is not to say that such differences are the fundamental reason for the hostility."

It is a mistake for Prager and Telushkin to ignore the persistence and universality of this phenomenon and to claim some special, more exalted, and elusive source of anti-Semitism, while half-denying the obvious and massively disproportionate representation of Jews in almost every index of human achievement. This evasive argument may reduce the number of available allies and divert attention from the real problem.

Prager and Telushkin are so immersed in the world of the Left and its perspectives that their economic analysis treats wealth or capitalist prowess as negatives, as potential sources of anti-Semitism from labor movements and the poor and their advocates, rather than as the best remedies for anti-Semitism.

Capitalism overthrows theories of zero-sum economics and dog-eat-dog survival of the fittest. Thus, as in the United States (except for the Darwinian academic arena, where professors angle for grants from the outside), anti-Semitism withers in wealthy capitalist countries. It waxes in socialist regimes where Jews may arouse resentment because of their agility in finding economic niches among the interstices of bureaucracies, tax collections, political pork fests, and crony capitalism. As the elder Netanyahu's great history shows, an oft-repeated pattern has the Jews serving as the most skilled and trusted servants of the central (or even absentee) government. Then, as the power of the hated king or conqueror wanes, he abandons the Jews, who are left to the mercies of the enraged mob.

Static socialist or feudalistic systems, particularly when oil-rich and politically controlled, favor a conspiratorial view of history and economics. Anti-Semitism is chiefly a zero-sum disease.

Christians may well be appalled by Prager and Telushkin's accounts of the depraved anti-Semitism of Martin Luther, various miscreant cardinals, and rabid crusaders, as capitalists will abhor the views of Henry Ford. And all the charges are true. But, putting it as gently as I can, I would demur at the retrospective application of modern standards of morality to the long history of the human parade through the treacherous and bloodthirsty epochs of war, poverty, religious feuds, plagues, famines, and vicious ethnic struggles. The world has been at war for millennia, with hatred and death inherent on all sides. During World War I, an entire generation comprising approximately twenty million young European men was lost. After World War I, an additional twenty-nine million more Europeans died because of an influenza epidemic alone. Until the ascent of capitalism and trade, there was no alternative to joining in the zero-sum struggles for existence against enemies everywhere.

Feminists look back on that panorama and see nothing but misogynist oppression, rape, and murder. Blacks look back and see virtually nothing but lynching and slavery. Native Americans see nothing but genocidal aggression by whites. Third Worlders everywhere see a history of colonialist and imperialist depredations. Armenians and Kurds give harrowing accounts of a history of murderous attacks that killed millions of their forebears. The Irish see an inexorable saga of predatory and vicious Englishmen, callously starving their ancestors to death. American Southerners tell of the loss of a generation of young men and the devastation of Dixie in the "War between the States." The Muslims tell of rampant brutalities of the Crusades. All of them cherish their own acute grievances and sagas of victimization. All now have been taught to couch their historic suffering, whenever possible and often even when implausible, in the terms of "genocide."

It is unseemly, as well as tactically questionable, for American Jews, the richest people on earth, to grapple with Armenians and Rwandan Tutsis, Palestinian Arabs and American blacks, Sudanese and Native Americans to corner the trump cards of victimization. Although Jews are objectively correct that the Holocaust was unique in its diabolical details and genocidal reach, current-day Jews will get nowhere pointing to the suffering of their forebears. Every ethnic group has its own tale of woe, because the entire history of the world is woebegone. For most of human history, average longevity was under thirty years. For the vast majority of humans of all ethnic groups, nearly all previous history seemed essentially hopeless in any terms except the physical struggles for Darwinian group survival. You hated your enemies from other groups because most of the time they sought to kill you. You had no vision of the successes of others as opening the doors of opportunity for you.

Until the dominance of capitalism, with its positive spirals of mutual gain, the prevailing regime was a Darwinian zero-sum game in which groups fought for survival against their neighbors. As Walter Lippmann eloquently explained in *The Good Society*, capitalism for the first time opened a vista of mutually enriching enterprise, with the good fortune of others providing opportunities for all. The Golden Rule, he said, was transformed from an idealistic vision of heaven into a practical agenda. From *Poor Richard's Almanack* to rich Andrew Carnegie's autobiographical parables, all were rediscovering the edifying insights of the author of Proverbs.

Yes, "Jew-hatred is unique," as Prager and Telushkin's first chapter announces. Jews are unique. Anti-Semitism subjects this uniquely gifted people to a crude and particularly incendiary manifestation of the immemorial hatreds that have afflicted the world for millennia. Judaism, however, perhaps more than any other religion, favors capitalist activity and provides a rigorous moral framework for it. It is based on a monotheistic affirmation that God is good and will prevail through transcending envy and hatred and zero-sum fantasies. Judaism can be plausibly interpreted as affirming the possibilities of creativity and collaboration on the frontiers of a capitalist economy.

The facts are clear. What makes Jews unique is their excellence. The solution is also clear. As Prager and Telushkin acknowledge, almost in passing, Jews do better under capitalism than under any other system. Anti-Semitism tends to wane under a growing and expanding creative economy. Other consequences of Jewish superiority are also evident. On a planet where human life subsists upon the achievements of human intellect and enterprise, Jews are crucial to the future of the race.

The Holocaust was not only an unspeakable catastrophe for Jews and an eternal source of shame upon all who collaborated with the Nazis' "final solution." It was also incomparably more destructive than other modern genocidal acts not only because of the diabolical evil of the Nazis but because of the unique virtues and genius of its victims. It was an irretrievable loss and catastrophe for all humanity, depleting the entire species of intellectual resources that are critical to survival on an ever-threatened planet.

As irremediable and tragic the loss to the Jewish people and all Jewish families directly affected by the Holocaust, one could argue that the rest of the world has suffered even more in absolute terms by the loss of the vast potential of the six million Jewish victims whose only sin was being Jewish on the European continent in the twentieth century.

The incontestable facts of Jewish excellence constitute a universal test not only for anti-Semitism but also for liberty and the justice of the civil order. The success or failure of any minority in a given country is the best index of its freedoms. In any free society, Jews will tend to be represented disproportionately in the highest ranks of both its culture and its commerce. Americans should not conceal the triumphs of Jews on our shores but celebrate them as evidence of the superior freedoms of the US economy and culture.

The real case for Israel is incomparably more potent and important than the sentimental and self-serving mush usually mustered on its behalf. It has little or nothing to do with Israel's murky politics, its frequently malfunctioning democracy, its extraordinary restraint in the face of constant provocations from its seething circle of demented neighbors, its treatment of gays or Palestinians or women or ethnic minorities, or its maddening indulgence of the socialist sophistries of its critics and casuistically captious friends at Harvard, the *Atlantic*, and the *New York Times*.

The prevailing muddle of sentimentality and pettifoggery only obscures the actual eminently practical case for supporting Israel, for as long as it may take, without apology or deceit or waffles, without deception or obsequious self-denial. It is the case for Israel as the leader of human civilization, technological progress, and scientific advance. It is the case for Israel as a military spearhead of the culture of freedom and faith—the bastion of American progress and prosperity, and beyond America, for the progress and prosperity of all the people of the planet. The reason America should continue to "prop up" Israel is that Israel itself is a crucial prop of American wealth, freedom, and power, as well as standing strong on the front lines of the Western battle against its intifada [Arabic for "uprising"]-besotted enemies.

In a dangerous world, faced with an array of perils, the Israel test asks whether the world can manage to suppress its envy and recognize its dependence on the outstanding performance of relatively few men and women. The world does not subsist on zero-sum legal niceties. It subsists on hard and potentially reversible accomplishments in medicine, technology, pharmacology, science, engineering, and enterprise. It thrives not on forcibly reallocating land and resources but on encouraging and giving freedom to human creativity in ways that exploit land and resources most productively. The survival of the human race depends on recognizing excellence wherever it appears and nurturing it until it prevails. It relies on a vanguard of visionary creators on the frontiers of knowledge and accomplishment. It depends on passing the Israel Test.

Critics will call this a culpably Judeo-centric argument, missing lots of subtleties and complexities that shrewd, tough-loving critics of Israel cherish in their long catalog of its flaws. Former Prime Minister Ehud Olmert had the best answer, assuring writer Jeffrey Goldberg of the *Atlantic* that he did not care about the flaws. Regardless of flaws— and Israel has fewer flaws than perhaps any other nation—Israel is the pivot, the axis, the litmus, the trial. Are you for civilization or barbarism, life or death, wealth or envy? Are you an exponent of excellence and accomplishment or of a leveling creed of troglodytic frenzy and hatred?

CHAPTER THREE

THE ECONOMICS
OF SETTLEMENT

A prime cause of Mideast tensions and turmoil, according to the international media, are Israeli "settlers." According to the prevailing "narrative," they are strange extremists who reside illegitimately in the "occupied territories" of the West Bank. Even such celebrated and fervent supporters of Israel as Alan Dershowitz and Bernard-Henri Levy deem the settlers beyond the pale of their Zionist sympathies.

As is his wont, Lester Brown of the Worldwatch Institute adds to these political concerns a coming environmental catastrophe, also presumably aggravated by the Israeli settlers and their hydrophilic irrigation projects. He sees the Middle East as direly threatened by the growth of population and the exhaustion of water resources. The Worldwatch Institute explains: "Since one ton of grain represents 1,000 tons of water, [importing grain] becomes the most efficient way to import water. Last year, Iran imported 7 million tons of wheat, eclipsing Japan to become the world's leading wheat importer. This year, Egypt is also projected to move ahead of Japan. The water required to produce the grain and other foodstuffs imported into [the region] last year was roughly equal to the annual flow of the Nile River."

Although these two concerns might seem unrelated, they converge in the history of Israel, a modern nation-state created by several generations of settlers and constrained at every point by the dearth of water in a predominantly desert land. In the mid-nineteenth century, before the arrival of the first groups of Jewish settlers fleeing pogroms in Russia and Ukraine, Arabs living in the British Mandate of Palestine—now Israel, the West Bank, and Gaza—numbered between 200,000 and 300,000. Their population density and longevity resembled today's conditions in parched and depopulated Saharan Chad. Although Worldwatch might prefer to see the Middle East returned to the more Earth-friendly and sustainable demographics of Chad, the fact that some 13.2 million Arabs now live in the former British Mandate, with a life expectancy of 77.5 years, is mainly attributable, for better or worse, to the work of those Jewish settlers.

Chronicling the origins of this Jewish feat in 1939, nine years before the creation of the modern State of Israel, was one of the little-known heroes of the twentieth century, Walter Clay Lowdermilk. An American expert on land usage, he formulated and popularized the most successful techniques of soil reclamation and watershed management around the globe. Today the Department of Agricultural Engineering of Technion University in Israel bears the lapidary name of this American Christian, and the world-leading feats of Israeli water conservation attest in part to the lasting power of his influential books.

A Rhodes Scholar at Oxford who went on to earn his doctorate in forestry and geology at Berkeley, Lowdermilk focused on "reading the land" for its tales of human civilization. He gauged cultures by their successes and failures in expanding the land's capacity to sustain human life. A slim US Department of Agriculture volume with a grand title, *Conquest of the Land through 7000 Years*, summarized many of his findings in 1953. It sold millions of copies and shaped the views of several generations of soil conservationists.

Married to a Christian missionary, Lowdermilk joined the faculty at Nanking University in northern China early in his career to find remedies for the great famine there in 1920 and 1921. Rejecting the prevailing theory of climate change as the cause of the tragedy, Lowdermilk and his Chinese colleagues identified the real culprit to be the enormous load of silt borne down the Yellow River every year. Deposited in the lowlands of the river, it caused floods on the plains and depleted the up-country of soils. "In the presence of such tragic scenes," he wrote, "I resolved to devote my lifetime to study of ways to conserve the lands on which mankind depends."

Becoming assistant chief in charge of research for the US Soil Conservation Service (now part of the US Department of Agriculture) in 1938 he embarked on a global mission to determine how the experience of older civilizations could guide the US in surmounting its own agricultural crises of the dust bowl and the gullied soil erosion in the South. This 25,000-mile peregrination ended in the British Mandate of Palestine, where he confronted the question of how the "land flowing with milk and honey" described in the Bible had become a wasteland.

In ancient times, as he knew, the region was largely self-sufficient, with a population of millions, producing four staples for export—olive oil from the hills, wine from the plains, dates from the Jordan Valley, and grains, chiefly from Trans Jordan. Replete with forests, and teeming with sheep and goats, the landscape evoked the plenitude of the European Mediterranean basin.

As Lowdermilk observed, the British Mandate territory, though far smaller in area, is topographically similar to Southern California. "The outstanding difference between the two areas is their geological structure," Lowdermilk found, "and in this respect Palestine is more favored," with better soils and affluent springs in its mountain valleys.

By 1939, however, when Lowdermilk arrived in the territory, it was largely an environmental disaster. As he recounted in his 1944 book *Palestine, Land of Promise*, "when Jewish colonists first began their work in 1882...the soils were eroded off the uplands to bedrock over fully one half the hills; streams across the coastal plain were choked with erosional debris from the hills to form pestilential marshes infested with dreaded malaria; the fair cities and elaborate works of ancient times were left in doleful ruins." Thousands of abandoned village sites pocked the countryside as Hebrew, Greco-Roman, and Byzantine periods of prosperity, with their populations of millions, had given way to waste and ruin and radical population decline under Muslims after 1100AD. By 1931, in the most reliable census the British took of a larger expanse of Palestine (including parts of Lebanon), the land held somewhere around a million people, less than one tenth of today's population in Israel and the current territories. Around the current Tel Aviv, Lowdermilk was told "no more than 100 miserable families lived in huts." Jericho, once shaded by luxuriant balsams, was treeless.

Lowdermilk wrote, "Those who can read the record that has been written in the land know that this state of decadence is not normal." As the Jerusalem native and Arab traveler Al-Mukaddasi had reported during the tenth century, Palestine was a fecund land of industry and agriculture, famous for its marble quarries and its "incomparable quinces." But Arab invaders from the desert brought a primitive culture that destroyed agriculture and eventually plunged Palestine into its "age of darkness."

"During most of the past 1200 years," Lowdermilk wrote, "lands of the Near East have been gradually wasting away; its cities and works have fallen into neglect and ruin; its peoples also slipped backward into a state of utter decline." The decay reached its nadir during "the four centuries of Turkish rule, from 1517 to 1918," with "appallingly high taxes on every tree and vine, leading to a treeless wasteland."

What amazed Lowdermilk, though—and changed his life—was not the 1,200-year deterioration, but the feats of reclamation in both highlands and lowlands accomplished by relatively small groups of Jewish settlers in only the five previous decades. As one of many examples of valley reclamation, he tells the story of the settlement of Petah Tikva, established by Jews from Jerusalem in 1878, in defiance of warnings from physicians who saw the area outside what is now Tel Aviv as hopelessly infested with malarial mosquitoes. After initial failures and retreats, Petah Tikva became "the first settlement to conquer the deadly foe of malaria," by "planting Eucalyptus [known locally as 'Jew trees'] in the swamps to absorb the moisture," draining other swamps, importing large quantities of quinine, and developing rich agriculture and citriculture.

By the time of Lowdermilk's visit, Petah Tikva had become the largest of the rural Jewish settlements," supporting 20,000 people, including the maternal side of Prime Minister Netanyahu's family, "where there were only 400 fever ridden *fellaheen* sixty years ago." (Today Petah Tikva is at the center of Israel's high-tech industry.)

The kibbutz of Kiriath Anavim, located in the gouged and gullied hills near Jerusalem, epitomized the miracle of soil reclamation by settlers—descended from a tiny group of immigrants from Ukraine. Founded in 1920 among thorn bushes, dwarfed trees, and a desolate rubble of rocks, by the time of Lowdermilk's arrival, the settlement boasted elaborate terraced lands, orchards and vineyards, with plum, peach, and apricot trees, honey and poultry, together with prosperous dairies producing milk for Jerusalem and Tel Aviv.

In draining swamps, leaching saline soils, turning the driest of sand dunes into orchards and poultry farms, in planting millions of trees on rocky hills, building elaborate water works and terraces on the hills, digging 548 wells that supplied irrigational canals for thousands of acres in little over a decade—as well as establishing industries, hospitals, clinics, schools—the half-million Jewish settlers massively expanded the economic, social, and agricultural capacities of the land. It was these advances that both attracted and enabled the fivefold twentieth-century surge of the area's Arab population by 1940.

As Lowdermilk recounted it, in the twenty-one years between 1921 and 1942, the Jews had increased the number of enterprises fourfold, the number of jobs more than tenfold, and total invested capital from a basis of a few hundred thousand dollars to the equivalent of $70 million in 1942 dollars (or $1.3 billion in 2024 dollars.) During the 1930s, the Palestine

Electric Company, founded in 1923 by Pinchas Rutenberg with financial support from the Rothschilds, increased output of kilowatt hours from 11.5 million to 103 million, raising the standard of living to a new level. Jewish technologists and skilled workers even built road networks in Syria, a bridge across the Euphrates in Iraq, and the innovative refineries of the Anglo Persian Oil Company.

Particularly significant in Lowdermilk's view were the purchases of large expanses of unused Arab land by Jewish settlers, many of whom had earned the necessary funds by their own hard work on the arid soils, from the Arabs, who controlled large expanses of untilled land. On most occasions, the settlers bought only a small proportion of a particular Arab holding. Since the Jews paid the Arabs three or four times what similar plots sold for in Syria (and far more even than in Southern California), the Jewish purchases provided capital for Arab farms, producing a dramatic expansion of their output. "In cases where the land belongs to absentee owners and tenants are forced to move...I found that the Jewish purchasers had provided compensation to enable the tenants to lease other property."

Lowdermilk reported that most Arab landowners had already begun to resist the Jewish improvements and to resent Jewish success, while the British in the area "are imbued with old colonial traditions and befriend [Arab] feudal leaders." European diplomats often enjoyed going native by mimicking Arab grandees in their flowing robes (who in turn were learning European ethnic prejudices and disdain for "men in trade"). Together they smeared these fully beneficial transformations of the region with anti-Semitic slurs and caricatures. However, the results of the purchases were clear: "During the last 25 years (before 1939), Jews have acquired just six percent of Palestine's 6.5 million acres or 400 thousand acres, less than one quarter of which was previously cultivated by Arabs." In three years between 1933 and 1936, Jews paid some $18 million for portions of Arab land, allowing Arabs to modernize their own farms and support major inflows of Arab immigration.

During this period of Jewish settlement before the creation of the modern State of Israel, opportunities in Palestine attracted hundreds of thousands of Arab immigrants from Iraq, Syria, Jordan, and the desert. Wages for Arab workers were double or more than the wages in Syria, Jordan, and Iraq. In 1936, a British Royal Commission concluded, "The whole range of public services has steadily developed to the benefit of the [Arab] fellaheen...the revenue for those services having been largely provided by the Jews."

According to Lowdermilk's data, during the fifty years between 1889 and 1939, the number of Jewish settlements rose from twenty-two to 252 and land under cultivation grew more than fivefold, from 75,000 acres to 400,000. The country emerged from a "backward low yielding agricultural economy, dependent on grains and olives, and is evolving toward a modern scientifically directed and richly diversified economy, with fruits, vegetables, poultry, and dairy products. Tractors and threshers replace wooden plows and flails." With milk sales surging from a million litres in 1924 to twenty-six million in 1941, and honey production up from 900,000 pounds in 1936 to an estimated five million pounds in the mid-1940s, Palestine was once again on its way to reclaiming the Promised Land of Exodus as "flowing with milk and honey."

Lowdermilk clinches the argument by a sophisticated comparison with conditions in Jordan. A country four times larger than the British Mandate of Palestine (including Sinai), Jordan partakes of the same mountain fold of mesozoic limestone, the same rich river plains, the same Rift Valley and highlands, the same mineral resources, the same climate, and a several times larger population in ancient times. "The fortunes of Trans-Jordan through three thousand years merge with those of Palestine because of the physiographic unity of the two areas draining into the Jordan Valley." But despite Jordan's endowment of fertile soil, its comparatively ample water and ideal climate, at the time of Lowdermilk's visit, its agricultural output and per capita consumption of imports was one-fifth that of Palestine while its population density was only one-tenth of Palestine's.

The only discernible difference was the absence of Jewish settlements in Jordan. Without Jewish settlements, Jordan was suffering heavy emigration (mostly to America and to the British Mandate itself) while the Mandate territory attracted increasing flows of immigrants, mostly clustering around the Jewish settlements. With Jewish advances in food production, medicine, and public hygiene, Arab health statistics increasingly converged with those of the settlers. While the Arab *birthrate* actually decreased by 10 percent, the death rate fell by one-third and infant mortality dropped 37 percent. The net result was an Arab annual population growth rate of 16.2 percent, the highest in the world (exclusive of immigration). Lowdermilk summed it up: "Rural Palestine is becoming less and less like Trans Jordan, Syria and Iraq and more like Denmark, Holland, and parts of the United States [Southern California]."

As Lowdermilk wrote, "If we are interested in the regeneration of man, let all the righteous forces on earth support these settlements in Palestine as a wholesome example for the backward Near East, and indeed, for all who seek to work out a permanent adjustment of people to their lands."

Against all these heroic advancements, however, a European-originated countercurrent was flowing, and was indeed, about to reach its crest in the grotesque anti-Semitic horrors of the following decade. Just as the boom of the 1980s in the territories was followed by an intifada in 1990, so the advances fostered by Jewish settlers brought the siege of riots and pillaging that came to be known as the "Arab Awakening" of 1936 and 1937. As widely reported by Lowdermilk and others on the scene, and affirmed by Winston Churchill, during the previous decade, "Fascist Italy and Nazi Germany were very active in fomenting Arab discontents."

"I often thought," wrote Lowdermilk, "of what would happen to the Jews of Palestine and to the country as a whole if Jewish immigration were effectively stopped and the land placed under full Arab control as envisaged in somewhat nebulous form by the British White Paper of May, 1939." The answer had already been given in 1937, by the Grand Mufti of Jerusalem, the most notable Palestinian leader, who soon enlisted in Hitler's cause and spent the war at his headquarters in Berlin. "All Jewish immigration should be prohibited," the Mufti said, "since the country could not even absorb the Jews who were already there." They would have to be removed by a process "kindly or painful as the case might be."

Lowdermilk made a prescient prediction based on the precedent of Iraq. When the British relinquished their mandate there, the Iraqi leaders vowed to protect the Assyrians, which was the Christian minority in the country. "Instead, the Assyrian Christians were slaughtered by Arabs of the Mufti's ilk who did not wish to 'assimilate or digest them.'"

Lowdermilk foresaw that "Arab rule in Palestine would...put an abrupt end to the reclamation work now being carried on so splendidly. Erosion would begin to have its way again in the fields. Peasant women in search of fuel and goats in search of pasture would make short work of the young forests."

Any end of Jewish immigration and settlement would mean a rapid end of Arab immigration and prosperity. Under Arab rule, Palestine had always been a somnolent desert land that could have sustained no authentic twentieth-century Arab awakening. Palestine without Jews is a not a nation but a *naqba*.

CHAPTER FOUR

THE PALESTINIAN ECONOMY

After World War II, when the surviving Jews of Europe fled to Palestine and what became the State of Israel, there was still no self-conscious Palestinian nation, no Arab industrial base, and virtually no exports other than oil. The Jews were not occupying a nation; they were building one.

Many people imagine that this new and larger influx of Jewish settlers after World War II perpetrated an injustice on the Arabs. But these Jews continued the heroic and ingenious pattern of development depicted before the war in 1939 by Lowdermilk and imparted the same massive benefits to the Palestinian Arabs.

With the Arab population growing apace with the Jewish population in most neighborhoods, and, indeed, even faster in some, no significant displacement could possibly have occurred. The numbers discredit as simply mythological or mendacious all the Palestinian grievance and eviction literature invented by the likes of Ilan Pappe, Avi Shlaim, Rashid Khalidi and scores of other divas of the *naqba* narrative. What took place, in fact, was the reclamation and enrichment of the land, and, as a consequence, a massive Arab migration to inhabit that land.

By 1948, the Arab population in the Mandate area had grown to some 1.35 million, up 60 percent since the 1930s, and up by a factor of seven since the arrival of the first creative cohort of Jews from Russia and what was then The Ukraine in the 1880s. Mostly concentrated in neighborhoods abutting the Zionist settlements, this Arab population was the largest in the history of Palestine. Only invasion by five Arab armies—and a desperate, courageous Israeli self-defense—drove out many of the Arabs, some 700,000. These Palestinian Arabs were chiefly evicted or urged to flee by their own Arab leaders in 1948 in a war that the Jews neither sought nor initiated. But the war's outcome inflicted no demographically perceptible hardship on the Palestinian Arabs. The creation of the State of Israel and the success of its thriving economy only served to accelerate Arab immigration into the area. Today Israel, Gaza, and the West Bank accommodate some 5.5 million Arabs, with a population density ten times that of Jordan.

After 1948, the history of Palestinian Arabs may be divided into three periods: the postwar period from Israel's founding through the war in 1967, before which Gaza and the Sinai Peninsula were under Egyptian rule, and the West Bank was ruled by Jordan; the period of Israeli administration of these territories between 1967 and 1990; and the recent era of the so-called "peace process" led by reality-denying international organizations and American presidents. As the foreign affairs scholar Michael Mandelbaum has written, "While the statistical details remain cloudy and have provoked scores of academic brawls and millipedes of footnotes, capturing the historic dynamics of population, economic growth, and foreign aid is a matter not of statistical minutiae but of orders of magnitude. The rough orders of magnitude, as exemplified the growth of the Arab population and its longevity, tell a story stunningly contrary to that purveyed through the conventional wisdom.

The only real Palestinian *naqba* came not in 1948 at the hands of Zionists, but in 1949, at the hands of foreign aid bureaucrats in the form of United Nations Relief and Works Agency for Palestine Refugees (UNRWA). In an unprecedented decision, applied to no other refugees on the face of the Earth, the UN extended its smothering embrace not only to the allegedly innocent Arab "victims" of the chaos of the 1948 war but also in perpetuity to all their descendants.

Like most welfare states, the UNRWA was formed less to provide for the good of its beneficiaries than to assuage the guilt of its creators. In a desire to compensate the Palestinians for their alleged victimization by the creation of the State of Israel, the international bureaucracies perpetrated and created a genuine and permanent victimization. Masked by a roughly $4 billion annual flood of outside aid to the Palestinian Arabs, justified by flagrant fables of Arab displacement, and twisted by European and Third World bigotry toward Jews and capitalists, the UN work of worldly charity has wreaked six decades of moral havoc.

The UNRWA effectively granted its benefactions only on the condition that the Palestinians never relinquish their dream of the complete destruction of the State of Israel by violently displacing the Jews. Otherwise, these generations of putative Palestinians could hardly qualify as "refugees." Sixty years later, the UNRWA continues to underwrite and encourage murder, irredentism, terrorism, fecklessness, and futility among the 1.4 million hapless souls who live in its fifty-nine camps.

Financed by the United States and the European Union, as Michael S. Bernstam of Stanford's Hoover Institution explained in *Commentary* in December 2010, "UNRWA is still paying millions of refugees to perpetuate their refugee status, generation after generation, as they await their forcible return to the land inside the State of Israel.... UNRWA's institutionalization of refugee-cum-military camps is," wrote Bernstam, nothing less than "the principal obstacle to peace in the Middle East."

The UNRWA perpetuates the notion of a "right of return" to the land. Yet this land scarcely counted as a desirable asset or a prize to be awarded to anyone before the Jews reclaimed it and made its economy valuable and its land capable of supporting life. The refugees' forebears in many cases were more recent immigrants to Palestine than were the Jewish settlers.

"This is not the right of return," writes Bernstam, "it is a claim of the *right to retake*." But here even Bernstam slips on the rotten bananas of the conventional narrative. There is no retake or retrieval involved, but an utterly spurious claim of a right to seize the land from its lawful owners. "More than being detrimental to Israel, it is destructive for the Palestinians because it gives more belligerent groups, such as Hamas, an upper hand."

A typical harvest of misconceived foreign aid, this tragic error is at the heart of the Palestinian imbroglio and extends the Palestinian grievance beyond Gaza and the West Bank into countries such as Jordan, Syria, and Lebanon that also host Palestinian camps.

The invidious ideology of Palestinian victimization by Israel continues to guide the policies toward Israel in the majority of Western nations and in international organizations, blinding nearly all observers to the actual facts of economic life in the region. No one reading the literature could have any idea that throughout the three roughly twenty-year economic eras following 1948, the Palestinians continued to benefit heavily from Israeli enterprise and prospered mightily compared to Arabs in other countries in the region. The indispensable cause and precursor of Arab enrichment and population growth were always the enabling successes of Israeli settlers. Before the settlers, there was no growth and little Arab immigration to Palestine.

The true test of a culture is what it accomplishes in advancing the human cause—what it creates rather than what it claims. The late economist Lord Peter Bauer devoted much of his distinguished career to the study of the corrosive effects of foreign aid. What might be termed a "Bauer syndrome" prevailed nearly everywhere that foreign aid became the chief source of incremental income. Typically, foreign aid flows to governments and tends to increase the power of the recipient government in relation to the private sector. Thus, foreign aid fosters socialism, including, should the regime be so inclined, national socialism, and invariably, crony socialism.

As foreign aid eclipses entrepreneurial achievement as the dominant source of newfound income in a society, the influence of politics looms ever larger in the national life. A theater of grievance replaces a culture of economic advance. Displacing the peaceful outreach of commerce are seething concerns about domestic favoritism, international conspiracies, tribal loyalties, and personal betrayals. The more critical foreign aid becomes to a country's economy, the more it tends to foster violence between ethnic groups and political factions. This dynamic has governed much of the history of the Palestinians.

The first era of Palestinian economic history spanned the period between 1948 and 1967. During this period the Jordanians controlled the West Bank and the Egyptians controlled Gaza. In 1948, a total of nearly 600,000 Arabs lived in these Palestinian territories (not including those who remained in Israel proper). The most significant of these territories, the West Bank of the Jordan River (also known by its Biblical designations of Judea and Samaria), covers some 2,000 square miles of land. More than 500,000 Arabs lived in the West Bank in 1948. Gaza, the other territory, is a strip of land on the Mediterranean contiguous with Egypt, which is approximately twenty-five miles (forty kilometers) long and six miles (ten kilometers) wide that was home to almost 80,000 Arabs in 1948. As Hillel Halkin observed, "Jordan, Israel's main military adversary in 1948, saw to it that the West Bank it annexed had not a Jew in it." Similarly, Egypt would not permit Jews to live in Gaza.

In this first twenty-year phase, under Jordanian control, the Arab population of the West Bank increased by 20 percent, to some 600,000 by 1967, and the economy showed modest growth, with per capita income around $800. The population of Gaza rose fivefold to some 400,000, while the economy in Gaza stagnated under unofficial Egyptian rule and experienced an influx of Palestinian war refugees with their incumbent baggage of UN programs.

Many leading Palestinian entrepreneurs fled to Amman, Damascus, or Beirut, where they set up formidable machine shops and even banking and insurance firms. There are wealthy ex-Palestinians scattered throughout the Middle East. If economies are driven by the efforts of a relatively few exceptional entrepreneurs, most of the Palestinian "few" left their fellow Palestinians behind. Growth in the West Bank and Gaza was sluggish at best and no one in authority ever proposed the creation of an Arab Palestinian state beyond the one already established in Jordan.

The second era began after the 1967 war, when Israel routed the attacks of four hostile invading armies in six days. During this second period, Israel took over the West Bank and Gaza and administered its economy.

During the following twenty years under Israeli management until the First Intifada of 1987, the West Bank and Gaza comprised one of the most dynamic economies on the planet, with a decade of growth at a rate of roughly 25 percent per year from 1969 to 1979. Annual investment in constant dollars soared from less than $10 million in 1969 to some $600 million in 1991, rising from 10 percent of GDP to around 30 percent in 1987 (maintained through 1991). The Arab population rose from roughly one million in 1967 to almost three million in some 261 new towns. Despite the nearly triple growth in population, per capita income also tripled in the West Bank; and in Gaza, it rose from $80 to $1,706 from 1967 to 1987. Meanwhile, the number of Jewish settlers in the West Bank and Gaza increased only to 250,000.

During this period when the West Bank and Gaza were administered by Israel, the territories received little foreign aid, the economy boomed, and the Palestinians dramatically augmented their numbers, their business activity and their standard of living.

Efraim Karsh, who has been described by the scholar Daniel Pipes as the preeminent historian of the modern Middle East writing today, provides the details:

"At the inception of the occupation [in 1967], conditions in the territories were quite dire. Life expectancy was low; malnutrition, infectious diseases, and child mortality were rife; and the level of education was very poor. Prior to the 1967 war, fewer than 60 percent of all male adults had been employed, with unemployment among refugees running as high as 83 percent. Within a brief period after the war, Israeli occupation had led to dramatic improvements... [T]he number of Palestinians working in Israel rose from zero in 1967...to 109 thousand by 1986, accounting for 35 percent of the employed population of the West Bank and 45 percent in Gaza. Close to two thousand industrial plants, employing almost half of the work force, were established in the territories under Israeli rule.

"During the 1970s, the West Bank and Gaza constituted the fourth fastest-growing economy in the world...with per capita GDP expanding tenfold between 1968 and 1991...Life expect ancy rose from 48 years in 1967 to 72 in 2000...By 1986, 92.8 percent of the population...had electricity around the clock, as compared to 20.5 percent in 1967...[Similar advances occurred in hygiene, healthcare, child mortality, immunizations, and communications, which all rose to levels equal or exceeding other Middle Eastern countries]. The number of schoolchildren...grew by 102 percent...Even more dramatic was the progress in higher education. [From zero in 1967] by the early 1990s, there were seven [universities] boasting some 16,500 students."

This second era of Palestinian progress and prosperity came a cropper in 1987, when Palestinian Arab terrorists responded to the good fortune of their people the same way as they did in the 1930s. In a process dubbed by Western apologists as an "Arab Awakening," Arab leaders distracted the "street" with anti-Semitic chimeras. Fearing irrelevancy as hundreds of thousands of Palestinians collaborated with Jews, PLO agitators fomented the First Intifada, launching thousands of attacks on Israeli targets and putting economic growth into reverse.

Once again, the power of anti-Semitic politics, with international diplomatic gulls and gobblers in tow, overcame the upsurge of economic advance, delivering the Palestinian Arabs once again into the clutches of a rapacious gang of neo-Nazis. Thus began the woeful third era.

As Oussama Kanaan wrote in 1998 in the International Monetary Fund report, *Uncertainty Deters Private Investment in the West Bank and Gaza Strip*, "The Peace Process...had the potential to yield substantial welfare gains, largely through rapid growth in private investment...However, a look at the evolution of private investment since 1993 reveals a radically different and disturbing picture....In 1993–97 real private investment is estimated to have declined by an average of 10 percent per year and private investment's share in GDP to have declined from 19 percent of GDP in 1993 to 10 percent of GDP in 1997. What went wrong?"

The IMF report presents a raft of data from the dismal science to document the collapse. Although military measures to suppress the intifada did restrict economic activity, the real cause is the Bauer syndrome.

Previously, under Israeli administration, the Palestinians in the West Bank and Gaza were oriented toward the possibilities of enterprise and economic growth complementing Israel's own economy. For a decade, the territories represented a kind of unregulated "Wild East" for Israeli entrepreneurs and actually grew faster than Israel did. With Yasser Arafat banished, the Palestinians in the West Bank and Gaza enjoyed rapid economic growth in a climate of minimal violence.

Beginning in 1993, however, the United States and the United Nations essentially gave away the store to Arafat. Rehabilitated by the 1993 Oslo Accords, Arafat returned from his exile in Tunisia in July 1994, where he had fled from Lebanon in 1982. All the power—and money—flowed to the PLO's leader and from there to his personal, numbered Swiss bank account. With foreign aid pouring in by the billions to the terrorists, the result was the emergence of Hamas, battling Arafat's Fatah organization for power and perks and mobilizing the forces in Palestine out of favor with the PLO.

The increase in foreign aid after 1993 was associated with a 40 percent decline in per capita income in the first half of that decade together with mounting anti-Israel terrorism and anti-Semitic animus. As the PLO focused on politics and sedition, the Palestinian economy shrank, and dependence on foreign aid increased along with incessant complaints about the inadequacy of that aid. In this environment, Palestinian entrepreneurship collapsed amid much talk by Arafat and his minions of the "humiliation" of working for Jews.

From its outset early in the twentieth century, Palestinian nationalism itself was an artificial construct, characterized by hostility toward Jews, as well as toward capitalism. As the scholar, Michael Mandelbaum, has written, "Palestinian nationalism is the only one of the many nationalist movements that have appeared since the nineteenth century that has as its aim not the creation of its own nation-state but the destruction of another people." Palestinian political leaders were indifferent to enterprise and hostile to repeated international schemes for joint Arab–Israeli development of the Jordan River basin. Palestinian political behavior was so obnoxious that their leaders were rejected by every Arab state in which they sought refuge, including the contiguous and predominantly Palestinian state of Jordan when it ruled the West Bank between 1948 and 1967. But after 1967, and under Israeli rule, the Palestinians proved that by focusing on enterprise complementing the Israeli economy they could become prosperous.

• • •

In the face of this history, international organizations, from the World Bank to the United Nations Conference on Trade and Development (UNCTAD), have performed a series of further analyses of the Palestinian economy, including the experience of the Arabs within Israel. Their consensus is that foreign aid has been inadequate to meet the acute needs of the Palestinian Arabs. Meanwhile, the growth of the Israeli economy is ascribed largely to its exploitation of the Palestinians.

In essence, the growth of the Israeli economy emerges in these studies as the gigantic and intolerable "imbalance" in the region. This imbalance is seen to perpetrate huge "gaps." Contemplating this weighty matter, academic and political sages imagine that a more "balanced" outcome, gapwise, would be "a convergence of Israeli and Arab incomes in the area." The absence of such a convergence is somehow Israel's fault, or, for the more globally oriented, the fault of world capitalism.

In 1948, when Arabs comprised roughly 66 percent of the British Mandate of Palestine, their share of a national income of perhaps $2–$3 billion dollars was 40 percent. To an observer who views economic advance as a good thing, both enriching its entrepreneurs and providing economic opportunities for neighboring areas, the contributions of Zionism to the region would evince a need for yet more Zionist enterprise. This boon, in fact, occurred.

By 1992, the economy of Israel, including the predominantly Palestinian territories of the West Bank and Gaza, had grown to some $130 billion (in constant inflation-adjusted dollars). This forty-fold rise was accompanied by a near ten-fold rise in the output of the territories, to some $11 billion in constant dollars. By almost any standard, a ten-fold increase in real output over forty-three years is a considerable achievement, made to seem modest only by the extraordinary success of Israel.

Alas, 1992 would turn out to be the zenith for the Palestinian economy. The early 1990s saw a resurgence of suicide bombings, kidnappings, and missile attacks on Israel. The economic deterioration that began with the acceptance of the PLO as the official voice of the Palestinian cause after Oslo became real collapse with the so-called Second Intifada beginning in 2000. By the estimate of the World Bank, the economy of the territories had shrunk by some 40 percent in the first five years of the new millennium.

This acute downsizing occurred despite a continued influx of foreign aid from international bodies, a 20 percent rise in remissions from overseas Palestinians, and Israeli support and subsidies for the Palestinian Monetary Authority that was charged with upgrading banking in the Palestinian territories. Despite all this aid, however, per capita income in the territories continued to stagnate.

To the sages at the UN and in universities and think tanks, the diminution of the Palestinian economy was a result not of Palestinian violence under its rocket-rattling leaders but of Israeli restrictions on the free movement of Palestinians and impediments on their "access to natural resources." However, the most revealing gauge of the impact of the Israeli economy on Arabs—as opposed to self-inflicted disruption of terrorism—is the performance of the one-fifth of Palestinian Arabs who live in Israel as citizens.

A recent thicket of sociology was planted on the subject by the UN economist Raja Khalidi in the *Journal of Palestine Studies* published by the University of California Press in Berkeley, California, and edited by Khalidi's older brother, Rashid. Rashid Khalidi became briefly famous during Barack Obama's presidential campaign in 2008 for his "consistent reminders to me," as the presidential candidate said, "of my own blind spots and my own biases" related to Palestinian suffering. In his article, Raja Khalidi's view "pits a discriminatory and hegemonic Jewish state (and economy) against an ethno-national minority unable to access its fair share of national resources."

Concludes the UN guru: "The marginalization of Arabs in Israel is not unrelated to the state's Jewish character and its Zionist development policy preferences and priorities... [These] political, economic, and social processes... began well before 1948 and continue today to lock in and further degrade the position of Arabs [in Israel]."

"These gaps are not coincidences of history... rather, they emanate from distinct external processes that impede the free operation of theoretically perfect (but actually imperfect) markets. Although economic convergence in the long term is promised..." it requires "leveling the playing field"... both "between developed and developing countries" and in Israel.

There you have it all—"gaps" and "imbalances"; "economic convergence"; access to "natural resources"; unequal educational attainment; capital accumulation; playing-field leveling—and the old UN favorite since the days of Secretary General Raúl Prebisch of UNCTAD—deterioration of the "terms of trade" (the relative value of the goods and services exchanged between two political entities). In Israel's case, the terms of trade have supposedly shifted against Arabs peculiarly denied "access to natural resources,"—chiefly land—after they sold it to Israelis and suffered sellers' remorse. Apparently, they did not anticipate that the land (these "natural resources") could yield the region's most fertile farms and could give rise to skyscrapers and high-technology factories. Why didn't anyone tell them? Now they want it back, along with the skyscrapers and technologies.

The formidable successes of Palestinians working with Israel fail to impress Khalidi. According to him, Israel's own data on the Arab-Israeli economy "paint a dismal picture of the results of sixty years of failed integration (and Arab exclusion)." To rectify this Israeli failing requires "sustained policy intervention," if not by missiles and suicide bombers, then by the equally devastating ministrations of pious UN development officials. And there you also have the perennial social-ist invocation of "imperfections" in "theoretically perfect markets" to justify the eclipse of the market by managerial global bureaucrats and politicians.

Raja Khalidi's entire argument itself suffers from a huge gap—namely, the absence of a scintilla of evidence that Arabs anywhere in the world other than in the United States, have performed as well economically as the Arabs in Israel. Contrary to the claims of deterioration and "lock in," the Arab average annual per capita income in Israel is $600 per month (i.e., an annual household income of $14,400 for a family of four). This compares with an average annual income of $9,400 for a family of four in sparsely-populated Jordan, which roughly matches the average throughout the Arab world. Moreover, while Palestinians in the Gaza and the West Bank have undergone a catastrophic drop in income since the PLO's resurgence, the income gap between Israel's Palestinian Arab population and Jewish population has actually been declining. Some of the difference reflects the greater youthfulness and lesser workforce participation of Arab families. By the ultimate measure of longevity, Arabs in Israel are thriving, with a life expectancy growing over the past forty years from about fifty-two years to more than seventy-seven years.

Moreover, any income gap between the Jewish and Arab populations of Israel is clearly attributable to the prowess of Jewish entrepreneurs and other professionals, whose emphasis on higher education and professional achievement produces similar gaps in every free country on earth with significant numbers of Jews. Jews, for example, outearn other Caucasians in the United States by an even larger margin than they outearn Arabs in Israel. This probably reflects the fact that the United States used to have a freer economy, by most standards, than Israel.

Amid all the dismal talk of lock in and privation, even the UN guru Khalidi is compelled to acknowledge that "proximity to the more advanced Jewish economy has allowed for 'gains' [the quotation marks are Khalidi's] that many Palestinians living under occupation or in exile would envy." But to the UN economist, who wants to have it every which way, the so-called economic gains mask a "degradation of *social capital*" [emphasis added] because successful Arabs in Israel may be lured away from the jihad. The discreetly bloodthirsty UN sage thinks that what would help more than wealth and longevity is for the "Palestinian minority" to "succeed in mobilizing itself and its full weight within the Israeli-Palestinian-Arab conflict."

Khalidi's gingerly attitude of suspicion toward successful Arabs in Israel who may not share his political obsessions reflects the unwillingness of the quango economic establishment to recognize the one major obvious fact that looms over all their endless data. Arabs constitute roughly 50 percent of the population of the entire Israeli-Palestinian area but contribute only 11 percent of its output, and that mostly in public-sector employment. Per capita income of Palestinians outside of Israel is roughly one half that of their counterparts within Israel. Following the surging growth of the Palestinian economy during the second era under Israeli auspices, these statistics on the performance of Israeli Arabs suggest that nothing would benefit Palestinian Arabs more than an Israeli takeover of the entire territory from the Jordan River to the sea.

More important than all the political, economic, and legal debates, however, is the attitude toward achievement that is expressed in the literature of the Palestinian apologists. Most of it echoes the view of Arab leader Musa Alami, meeting with Ben-Gurion in 1934. When Ben-Gurion told him that Zionism "would bring a blessing to the Arabs of Palestine, and they have no good cause to oppose us" Alami replied, "I would prefer that the country remain impoverished and barren for another hundred years, until we ourselves are able to develop it on our own." This sentiment continues today under Hamas. In 2005, when Israelis actually relinquished their advanced greenhouses and irrigation equipment in Gaza, the leaders of Hamas ordered many of these facilities destroyed. Some things never change. On April 9, 2011, the PLO's chief representative in the United States, Maen Areikat, told the Jewish *Forward*: "Palestinians are not after improving their condition of living. Our real problem is ending the occupation"—getting rid of those dastardly settlers!

This concept of economic self-sufficiency is the chief cause of poverty in the world. No one can be rich alone. Wealth is the result of sharing and collaboration between an elite of capitalists and the insurgent new businesses rising up around them. It is a product of the willingness of the young and less-educated or less talented to work for the educated and able. It is a consequence of apprenticeship and learning followed by entrepreneurial rivalry. The success of the Israeli economy is not an imbalance that creates invidious gaps. It is a gap—that is, an opportunity—that summons new energies and new wealth.

All capitalist advances generate imbalances and disequilibriums. Growth is a ramification of the disequilibrating activities of entrepreneurs, the creative destruction unleashed by rare feats of extraordinary achievement. It is the fallacy of perfect competition and convergence that leads most of the global media and academic establishment *wunderkinder* to interpret as gaps and imbalances what in fact represents luminous achievement and creativity.

Emerging today is yet a fourth era for the Palestinian economy. The immediate prospects look grim. After the Gaza war of early 2009, the response of the international community was to mobilize some $4 billion in new foreign aid, including $900 million from the United States. Most of the money will tend to gravitate toward governmental institutions, increasing their relative power and discouraging the private economy of entrepreneurial energies. Dominant in Gaza and bristling with weapons, Hamas captures the bulk of these funds, regardless of the intentions of the donors. Hamas accepts the money as a well-earned reward for its missile attacks on Israel and will bask in their glow as the cycle of Western appeasement and Western pelf for terrorists continues. Like Arafat before them, the leaders of Hamas squirrel away aid money intended for the Palestinians into private bank accounts of their own.

Nonetheless, the long-term possibilities illuminated during the second era of Palestinian prosperity between 1967 and 1987 have become even more inviting with the new global ascendancy of the Israeli economy. Israel's current administration, under the business-savvy leadership of Benjamin Netanyahu, is committed to the economics of collaboration and prosperity. When the violence abates, he is resolved to open up new opportunities for Palestinian entrepreneurship and growth.

As always, the choice remains clear between the ascent of capitalism and freedom and the economics of dependency and the politics of national socialism.

So what does this history have to do with the Worldwatch Institute's alarms about a rising threat of water exhaustion in the Middle East? A few simple statistics suggest that the Israeli settlers (and, after all, to the Palestinian Authority, all Israelis are settlers) are the solution rather than the problem in the region. Since the foundation of the State of Israel in a land that is half desert with no rain during six months of the year, the population has risen tenfold. While the amount of land under cultivation has nearly tripled, agricultural production has increased sixteen-fold, producing some $2.45 billion worth of Israeli farm exports in 2021. At the same time, industrial output has surged some fifty-fold. Meanwhile, Israeli use of water has *decreased* by 10 percent.

Israelis now purify and recycle some 95 percent of the nation's sewage, including imports of *sewage* from the West Bank and Gaza—"They sell us sewage and we give them potable water," said one Israeli official. Israel is pioneering ever more efficient forms of drip irrigation and gains some 50 percent of its water from world-leading desalinization plants. With an array of new hydrological innovations, Israel provides the crucial answers to the acute water crisis that afflicts the Middle East and much of the rest of the world. Just as the Israeli settlers enabled the emergence of an economy in Palestine, so they offer the prospect of saving the entire Middle East from water exhaustion and poverty after the oil boom ends.

Israel's settlers are far less a problem than a solution to all the most acute problems of the Middle East. Progress toward peace would be expedited if an American government could recognize this supreme and basic fact of life in the region and could thus understand the sources of the economy of hate.

CHAPTER FIVE

THE ECONOMICS OF HATE

In a great prophetic work, "A Draft of Guidelines for the Reconstruction of Austria," written in May 1940 as a report for Otto von Hapsburg, the former archduke of Austria, economist Ludwig von Mises predicted the effects of the banishment of Jews from Austria after the Nazi annexation in 1938. By implication, he also foreshadowed the predicament of the Palestinians today.

Presenting the facts of life for small countries without oil or other valuable natural endowment, von Mises wrote: "As a mountainous country with poor soil and few natural resources, Austria must rely on industrial activity to feed a population of six and a half million people. As an agrarian nation, [it] could at best eke out enough food for a population of one to two million... To be an industrial country requires being predominantly an importer of raw materials and food and an exporter of industrial products...

"The mainstays of such an organism," von Mises pointed out, "are the entrepreneurs of the export industry who have the know-how to produce [competitive] goods for the world market. The industrial and commercial genius of these entrepreneurs creates work and livelihood for all the other citizens."

By von Mises's estimate, "Old Austria produced about one thousand men of this kind." Von Mises recognized what David C. McClelland saw in America in his *Achieving Society* and what Edward Roberts and

Charles Eesley discovered in "Entrepreneurial Impact" among MIT graduates. The leading entrepreneurial talent of the world is disproportionately Jewish. As von Mises observed about the entrepreneurs of the once-flourishing Austrian economy: "At least two-thirds of these one thousand men were Jews...They are gone, scattered around the world, and trying to start again from scratch."

Not only Jewish entrepreneurs were driven out of the Austrian economy. The hatred of Jews epitomized a general resentment of excellence and creativity. "Tax offices [as instruments of redistribution] were filled with a blind hate against 'plutocrats'" of all races and creeds. Moreover, technical talent and middle management were a crucial complement to entrepreneurial genius. Much of the most productive middle management of Austrian companies was also Jewish. Of the some 250,000 Jews in Austria in 1938, according to von Mises, a mere 216 individual Jews survived the war without leaving the country.

Von Mises concluded: "The so-called Aryanization of firms was based on the Marxist idea that capital (resources and equipment) and labor...were the only vital ingredients of an enterprise, whereas the entrepreneur was an exploiter. An enterprise without entrepreneurial spirit and creativity, however, is nothing more than a pile of rubbish and old iron." Austria was left with many piles of rubbish and old iron. Its newly *Judenrein* industrial economy, once an economic miracle of export-led growth and a paragon of European commerce, would never recover its leading role.

Growing up in Austria during the period described by von Mises was Adolf Hitler, whose original surname was Schicklgruber. Explaining this Austrian catastrophe and similar disasters in Hungary is the set of ideas and assumptions in Hitler's personal manifesto, *Mein Kampf*. Autobiography, creedal testament, anti-Jewish *cri de coeur*, and National Socialist agenda, Hitler's book is a dense, tortuous, and repetitious screed, suitable for consignment to the dustbins of history like its demonic author.

Mein Kampf, however, is anything but a historical relic. Banned by the Israelis when they governed the West Bank, it became popular there when the Palestinian Authority took over. With every new Arabic edition, it crops up on bestseller lists and bookstore displays across the Middle East. It loomed in menacing piles in the airport bookstore in Jordan. Israeli soldiers rooting through Arafat's possessions abandoned in southern Lebanon in 1982 discovered many copies at all his base camps. Its fevered references to "pigs"..."jackals"..."bacteria"..."vampires"..."parasites"..."vermin"...and "vultures" recurred in the speeches of Osama bin Laden of al-Qaida, former Iranian President Mahmoud Ahmadinejad, former Malaysian premier Mahathir Mohamad, and thousands of imams throughout Islamic lands, not to mention on college campuses and street protests in the West, where ignorance triumphs over knowledge.

As familiar and consequential as this book is, it is strangely misunderstood. It has been reviewed thousands of times without any grasp of the central theme of its case against the Jews. Critics notice the references to Jews as "an inferior race...the incarnation of Satan and the symbol of evil." Cited are Hitler's rage at the Jewish mastery of the press, manipulation of propaganda and public opinion, and the Jew's devious "benevolence" and charity as "manure" applied as fertilizer for "future returns." Critics comment upon Hitler's celebration of the *Protocols of the Learned Elders of Zion,* now ubiquitous in the Arab world, and that book's claims of an insidious Masonic conspiracy controlled by Jews throughout history. Hitler's antipathy toward the Jews emerges as a bizarre and phantasmagorical obsession, as a demented chimera, or as a paranoid fantasy unrelated to the sophisticated attitudes toward Israel and Jews now widely upheld in faculty lounges, international organizations, television talk shows, and noted journals of opinion and newspapers of record.

To Hitler, however, Jews are anathema, not chiefly because of such exotic figments as their alleged racial inferiority or their demonic Satanism or their perennial Masonic intrigues, but because of a far more common and fashionable complaint still widely voiced at Harvard,

Berkeley, and around the globe. Hitler's case against the Jews focuses on their mastery of capitalism.

As von Mises observed, more than two-thirds of the leading entrepreneurs in Austria at the time were Jewish. The focus of Hitler's racial theory in chapters ten and eleven of *Mein Kampf* is his resentment and paranoia toward Jewish prowess in finance and enterprise. The Jew's "commercial cunning...made him superior in this field to the Aryans," he wrote, and turned "finance and trade" into "his complete monopoly.... The Jew...organized capitalistic methods of exploitation to their ultimate degree of efficiency."

In a theme later adopted by Osama bin Laden, Hitler asserts that the key to initial Jewish success was "his usurious rate of interest." He cites the immemorial notion that Jews gain an economic foothold by mulcting others through their prowess as shysters and shylocks, ensnaring "ingenuous" Aryans in webs of debt. Blind to the nature of capitalism, Hitler condemns interest as illegitimate gain, the embezzled returns of dispensable middlemen. Then he makes an elaborate case that Jews parlay their sinister middleman strategies into a broader economic dominance, first in banking and finance and then in all of commerce and industry. He implies that their resulting affluence and ostentation will ultimately bring them down. Projecting onto others his own revulsion, Hitler contended: "The increasing impudence which the Jew began to manifest all round stirred up popular indignation, while his display of wealth gave rise to popular envy."

Adumbrating John Mearsheimer and Stephen Walt (both noted critics of Israel) on Jewish lobbying prowess, Hitler spoke of the Jew as an "eternal profiteer," who mitigated popular hostility by paying "court to governments with servile flattery [and] used his money to ingratiate himself further."

While sneering at Jewish lack of connection to the soil, Hitler wrote: "The cup of [Jewish] iniquity became full to the brim when he included landed property among his commercial wares and degraded the soil to the level of a market commodity. Since he himself never cultivated the soil but considered it as an object to be exploited, on which the peasant may still remain but only on condition that he submits to the most heartless exactions of his new master." This theme now pervades facile journalist coverage of the Palestinian territories, where water for agriculture is allocated chiefly to Jewish farms that pay for it by profitable use of the irrigated land.

Referring to Zionism, Hitler wrote, "They have not the slightest intention of building up a Jewish State in Palestine so as to live in it. What they really are aiming at is to establish a central organization for their international swindling and cheating," which is Hitler's characterization of Jewish enterprise.

Continuing his crude Marxist narrative, Hitler argues that as the Jews compiled wealth, "they bought up stock" in companies and had "predominance in the stock exchange." They "thus pushed [their] influence into the circuit of national production, making this...an object of buying and selling on the stock exchange...thus ruining the basis on which personal proprietorship alone is possible... [and creating] that feeling of estrangement between employers and employees...which led at a later date to the political class struggle."

This vision of a voracious and amoral capitalism that corrupts moral codes, exploits the environment, and degrades relations between workers and employers is a central theme of leftist economics today. Familiar, too, is the idea that stock and bond markets enable mostly Jewish middlemen and entrepreneurs, greenmailers and junk bond manipulators to seize companies from honest and stable management for financial exploitation. Change the wording by deleting the references to Jews and inserting the names of financiers, such as Michael Milken, Carl Icahn, George Soros, Henry Kravis, Gary Winnick, et al., or even such categories as "junk bond kings" and "private equity predators," and present it all under the name of, say, Schicklgruber, and you will have an exemplary book for public consumption at American universities. Unfortunately for some of the above, these anti-capitalist prejudices, with their often inadvertently anti-Semitic undercurrents, also made their way from the American media into American courts. Michael Milken, for example, was accused of being a Ponzi schemer and predator, but within two decades the companies he financed were worth more than a trillion dollars. He was forced to plead guilty to a series of trivial clerical offenses by the prosecutor's threat to indict his totally innocent brother Lowell. The idea that behind every great fortune is a great crime joins anti-Semitism and anti-capitalism in the moronic and moralistic embrace that Hitler pioneered and epitomized.

Hitler's complaint probes still more deeply, however. He charges Jews with violating the deepest mandates of the Darwinian law of nature. The heart of Hitler's case against the Jews was that through their superiority over Aryans in capitalist finance and trade, they were bypassing the law of survival of the physically fittest. They had found an individualist route to power without making the sacrifices necessary to achieve collective strength as warriors. They were circumventing the mandate of nature that requires all creatures to gang together and fight for their own survival.

This is Hitler's concept of the key conflict in economies and societies. It is the division between Darwinian nature, governed by the survival of the physically fit and feral, and the effete and intellectual artifice of devious individualist entrepreneurs.

"Here we meet the insolent objection, which is Jewish in its inspiration and is typical of the modern pacifist. It says: 'Man can control even Nature.' There are millions who repeat by rote that piece of Jewish babble.

"Wherever [men] have reached a superior level of existence, it was not the result of following the ideas of crazy visionaries but by acknowledging and rigorously observing the iron laws of Nature."

This is the Hitler vision of the split between devious individuals (to him, Jewish) who gain power by prevailing in economic rivalry and groups that gain power by blood sacrifice in the perennial and always ultimately violent struggle for survival. It is the division between those who imagine that humans can manipulate nature and create new inventions under conditions of peace and those who believe that the greatest attainments come from solidarity and sacrifice in war.

As Hitler presents the law of nature in this way: "He who would live must fight. He who does not wish to fight in this world, where permanent struggle is the law of life, has not the right to exist."

As his devout jihadi followers do today, Hitler recognized that violence can trump economic exchange and progress. Against Jewish dominance in the stock market, he counterpoised his *Hitlerjugend*, or the malignant Hitler Youth movement, with its anti-Semitic lust for blood and its dominance in the streets. Just as the jihadis in their *madrasahs* today muster and indoctrinate a new generation of Islamic young males into Wahhabi codes of hatred and violence and suicidal martyrdom, Hitler's Brown Shirts espoused a solidarity with violence and sacrifice. Under a regime of "survival of the fittest," Hitler celebrated a sacrificial camaraderie and drive to war that could thwart the individual capitalist enrichment of Jews.

At the same time, to justify his own plans for mass exterminations, he blamed the Jews in Russia for perpetrating the starvation and massacre of thirty million Ukrainians, Kulaks, shopkeepers, and other "class enemies." (Reaching for the ultimate affront, he even charged: "The Jews were responsible for bringing Negroes into the Rhineland.")

Hitler portrayed envy and resentment of Jewish achievement as a campaign of vengeance and social justice. True "social justice," according to Hitler, "is a typical Aryan characteristic." Individualist to the core, Jews merely pretend to support equality and social justice. Marxism, for Hitler, is ersatz socialism contrived by Jews to mobilize the workers against the enemies of the Jews, such as his own impending National Socialist regime. But the deeper Jewish offenses that he primarily details and denounces in *Mein Kampf*—usury, stock manipulation, exploitation of the land, cunning in finance and trade—are all expressions not of cultural inferiority or Marxist machinations but of capitalist superiority.

When the Arab leader Musa Alami in 1934 told Ben-Gurion that he would prefer that Palestine remain a wasteland for a hundred years than permit the Israelis to develop it, he was echoing Hitler's position.

The fundamental conflict in the world pits the advocates of capitalist freedom, economic growth, prosperity, and property against the exponents of blood and soil and violence. Capitalism requires peace. A true capitalist wants war only against threats to international peace and trade.

Although everyone benefits from capitalist prosperity, it inexorably produces "gaps" between rich and poor. It necessarily requires toleration of superior entrepreneurs who can make the system work. A free regime will always tend to favor peoples who excel in commerce and industry. For centuries, Jews have been disproportionately represented among these entrepreneurs and inventors, scientists and creators. Even though Jews are a tiny minority of less than a tenth of 1 percent of the world's population, they comprise perhaps a quarter of the world's paramount capitalists and entrepreneurs. This was true at Hitler's time and it remains true today.

As in Hitler's time, demagogues tend to target successful capitalists for envy, resentment, and violence. They rant against the "rich" and wish to confiscate their wealth. They celebrate a cult of nature and land. In Thomas Friedman's admittedly felicitous metaphor, they cling to the olive tree and resent the Lexus. They hate capitalism and resent capitalists.

The ultimate source of their resentment is that, under capitalism, success does not normally go to the "best" or the naturally fittest as identified by physical strength or beauty or by the established criteria of virtue. Even the best in academic credentials do not prevail. To Hitler, "The Aryan...is the Prometheus of mankind, from whose shining brow the divine spark of genius has at all times flashed forth, always kindling anew that fire, which in the form of knowledge, illuminated the dark night by drawing aside the veil of mystery and thus showing man how to rise and become master over all the other beings on the earth." And so on. But if the Aryan's design of a Mercedes-Benz does not satisfy customers, he will not prevail over a member of the inferior Japanese race—making a Honda or a Toyota. If the Aryan's business choices do not prosper in the market, they will not succeed against the enterprises of Jewish entrepreneurs.

Under capitalism, Jews often prevail. Until the dominance of capitalism, Goths, Vandals, and Teutons prevailed. Hitler preferred the previous regime. Hitler's followers in the Middle East now wish to restore it.

CHAPTER SIX

THE ARCHETYPE
AND THE ALGORITHM

The twentieth-century descent of middle Europe into anti-Semitic mania, rage, and plutophobia brought down the Austrian and Hungarian economies and centers of culture. It built up the awesome animus and momentum of the Axis armies. It unleashed the frenzies of the Holocaust and the Stalinist pogroms and finally brought forth a new global empire and apparatus of Communist movements and powers. Then the forces mobilized by the Western democracies managed to turn back the totalitarian tide.

How did the Allied victory come about?

To observers who focus on politics and statecraft, the central history of the era follows the feats and follies of generals and dictators, politicians and demagogues. In many accounts, Roosevelt, Churchill, and Stalin, Eisenhower and Montgomery may seem to have defeated Hitler. But there is another way to tell the history of the time. All of these political and military leaders were utterly dependent upon the achievements of science and technology for their military success. At the same time that Hitler and Stalin, Roosevelt and Churchill were on center stage in the realms of statecraft and war, behind the scenes, other more singular and cerebral forces were quietly released into the world. They launched a countervailing tide that ultimately prevailed against Nazism and the Axis powers and ultimately overcame the communists as well.

Pushing this contrary tide was the Jewish diaspora. Flowing around the globe, devoid of the repulsive force of nationality, the largely homeless Jewish intellectuals honed in like neutrons into the nuclei of the most receptive centers of Western science and technology. There they galvanized the energies that won the war, shaped the peace, and transformed the global economy and the scientific culture of the age.

This process had begun early in the twentieth century. Before quantum theory, science was chiefly an enterprise of gentile Europeans—men like Isaac Newton, James Clerk Maxwell, Lord Kelvin, Ernest Rutherford, and Max Planck. With the rise of quantum theory came the ascendancy of Jews in science, led by Albert Einstein, Niels Bohr, Wolfgang Pauli, and Max Born. In the post-World War II era, Richard Feynman became the paramount teacher and interpreter of quantum theory.

The twenty-first-century world emerged chiefly from this microcosm: the new revelation of the early twentieth century that matter consisted not of unbreakable solids but of enigmatic waves of energy, largely governed by information. From quantum theory ultimately emerged IBM, Intel, Microsoft, Google, Sony, and Qualcomm. From quantum theory, too, would spring forth—from the wretched wastes of communism and feudal paralysis—the vast new energies of China, India, and the rest of increasingly capitalist Asia.

These developments originated in Europe early in the twentieth century, with events in Budapest and Vienna first rocking and then overturning the cradle of the new science and industry. The history of Budapest echoed the history of Vienna. In both great cities of the Hapsburg Empire, Jewish entrepreneurs led an economic miracle. But in science, Budapest was preeminent. From quantum mechanics to nuclear weapons to computer technology, information theory, and holography, Hungarian Jews bestrode the history of the twentieth century, from the pinnacles of research to the practical triumphs of Silicon Valley.

Paramount among these Hungarian Jews were Eugene Wigner, Edward Teller, and Leó Szilárd, who all played vital roles in the creation of nuclear weapons; Dennis Gabor, the Nobel laureate who invented holography; Michael Polanyi, the eminent chemist-philosopher who inspired a school of followers around the globe; and Arthur Koestler, the scientist-historian who wrote *Darkness at Noon* and edited *The God That Failed*, two books vital to the defeat of communism among intellectuals.

Of all the Jews who emerged from the anti-Semitic turmoil of Europe during World War II, however, none had more impact on the history of the epoch than the son of a marriage between Budapest banker Max Neumann and scion of finance, Margit Kann. Adding an aristocratic "von" from the title Max Neumann purchased in 1913 but never used himself, his son John's name became von Neumann and it looms over our history. Born on December 28, 1903, John von Neumann epitomizes the role of the Jews in the twentieth century and foreshadows their role in the twenty-first. Although he was not a religious Jew and I have been challenged for stressing his role, he was genetically and paradigmatically Jewish and his vision was virtually rabbinical in its rigorous drive toward ever more exalted abstraction and unity.

Von Neumann's record of accomplishment is as stunning as his ubiquity across the sciences of his era. But his record, like his ubiquity, can be deceptive. Von Neumann's work intrudes widely not so much because he was a man of many ideas but because he was a man of one idea, or perhaps one idea about ideas.

Assuming an intellectual position more exalted in the hierarchy of knowledge than perhaps any of his peers, he successively imposed his synoptic mastery of abstraction in mathematics, quantum mechanics, nuclear weapons, computer science, game theory, and information theory. Bringing all these sciences and capabilities to bear, he could be said to have tipped the balance in the cause of freedom. But as Eugene Wigner wrote in his autobiography, "Despite the variety, all of his very great achievements rose from a single coherent view of life." Since his childhood, von Neumann had been a master of the ladders of abstraction, from physical data through number and symbol to set and group, all unified by the concept of the algorithm.

An algorithm can be thought of as any step-by-step set of instructions that is sufficiently precise to produce a determined outcome in every iteration without additional human intervention. Any machine from which its human tenders can walk away while it does its job is driven by an algorithm, which can be abstracted from the machine itself. Men make algorithms, but they also discover them in the process of exploring the physical world. Not every human endeavor is algorithmic. The design of a pitching machine made by men is algorithmic; the prowess of a Major League Baseball pitcher is not. Not every natural process is or can be described algorithmically: the human genome is revealed increasingly as being within the algorithmic realm; along with many other complex and chaotic processes, global weather patterns still lie well outside it.

The algorithmic realm can be thought of as comprising all phenomena that can be satisfactorily governed or analyzed by some system of logic, from the somewhat stilted but still recognizably human language of much modern computer programming to the highest abstractions of mathematics.

The progress of science and technology into the algorithmic realm has depended on progress into the quantum realm. It was von Neumann, more than any other man of his era, who joined the two. We can delve deep into the atom only by rising up to a level of mathematical abstraction just glimpsed in the previous experimental science of the visible world.

But we do not, as von Neumann supremely understood, rise infinitely. As Kurt Gödel demonstrated in the early twentieth century, and von Neumann, as Gödel's first interpreter and greatest proponent, repeatedly demonstrated, the symbolic logic driving both math and science—the computer and the quantum—is ultimately axiomatic. It cannot prove itself in its own terms but must rely on a set of assumptions outside the system.

Though it frustrated many, von Neumann found this result both liberating and exhilarating. It would all be up to him. The limits of logic—the futility of the German titanic mathematician David Hilbert's quest for a hermetically sealed universal theory—would liberate human beings as creators. Gödel's incompleteness theorem emancipates man from determinism and makes logic a more powerful tool of human choice and creation. Reifying theory into practice, science into technology, becomes the role of human entrepreneurs and engineers.

Not only could humans discover algorithms, they also could compose them. This loophole in the mathematical logic of the universe would make von Neumann the most influential of all the great scientists of the twentieth century in the practical sphere.

Not only was a new science created, but also a new economy that, more than any other previous human achievement, affirmed the core of all capitalist morality and the basis of all sound political economy: wealth springs from the minds of human beings, and, above all, from the minds of the relatively few human beings who operate at the nexus of word and world—on the borders of math and manufacture—in the realm of the algorithm. The struggle against Marx and Hitler, as between the West and the jihad today, is best understood as a war between the denizens of the new realm and the rage of its enemies who cannot contribute to its genius. Hitler's claim in *Mein Kampf* that the Jews used commerce to cheat nature and deprive Aryans of the status due the warrior is a rant against the need to compete in the algorithmic realm. Fittingly, "Jewish science," in Hitler's derisive term, would become the decisive weapon in the war's military struggle, as it remains today.

Despite the enormous and indispensable role of non-Jews in the new realm, Hitler's jibe was on target. The most valorous feats of Jews and the vilest slanders against them arise from this recognition: as the level of abstraction rises in any arena of competition so does relative Jewish achievement. It is easier to observe (and attack) this anomaly than to explain it. Surely IQ, which mostly gauges the ability to perform abstract thought, is part of the explanation. But just as surely figuring in the causes is the diaspora's long history of exclusion from the "real" economy (as the materialists have always seen it), shunting Jews to the manipulative realms of trade, bookkeeping, shopkeeping, philosophy and finance. In any economy operating at its highest realm of abstraction, the allocation of capital can be among the most valuable kinds of work.

And it did not hurt that Jews have believed from before the fatherhood of Abraham that it was the word that made the world—the ultimate assertion of algorithmic power.

Norman Macrae's intense and inspirational biography of von Neumann tells the tortured story of the Budapest from which he emerged early in the century. As Macrae describes it: "In the three and a half decades before Johnny's birth in 1903, Budapest had been the fastest-growing big city in Europe—next to New York and Chicago, possibly the fastest in the world.... [in just eight years] freight traffic on Hungary's railroads rose from 3 million tons in 1886 to 275 million in 1894 and passenger traffic multiplied nearly seventeenfold." At the time of von Neumann's youth, industry was flourishing, with the number of industrial workers surging from 63,000 in 1896 to 177,000 by 1910. Between 1867 and 1903, the population of Budapest rose from 280,000 to more than 800,000, surpassing such cities as Rome, Madrid, Brussels, and Amsterdam.

Vienna's twin in the Hapsburg Empire, Budapest achieved these feats chiefly through the expedient of welcoming Jewish immigration. With virtually no Jews as late as 1867, Hungary accepted hundreds of thousands by the time of von Neumann's birth. At the time von Neumann entered the elite Lutheran High School in Budapest, 52 percent of the students were listed as Jewish. Perhaps two-thirds of the leading citizens of Budapest, outside the government—bankers, lawyers, industrialists, musicians, scientists, artists—were Jewish. Although they made up only five percent of the Hungarian population, they became the vanguard of Hungarian economy and culture.

Steve J. Heims' fascinating joint biography of von Neumann and his MIT rival, Norbert Wiener, *John von Neumann and Norbert Wiener: A Dual Biography*, expresses the fashionable view that the huge success of Jews in Hungary "often involved repudiation of their own origins and their less fortunate brothers...and was often achieved at great psychological cost." This psycho-sanctimony has become familiar on ivied campuses. But there is no evidence whatsoever that the success of the Jews who revitalized Hungary came at the expense of anyone else. In sophisticated form, Heims is expressing the usual cankered incomprehension of capitalism common among intellectuals everywhere, and, in cruder form, flagrant among other citizens as well, including many leftist Jews. It was such blindness to the wide benefits of Jewish achievement—and the resulting lethal resentment of Jewish wealth—that ultimately would drive the Jews away, bringing down the Hungarian economic boom along with the simultaneous, though less spectacular, economic rise in Austria.

Nonetheless, for most of von Neumann's youth, Budapest thrived. To eminent business families like the von Neumanns and Kanns, his forebears, the city must have seemed even more secure and idyllic than Beirut seemed to Christians before the eruption of its fifteen-year civil war, triggered by Arafat's choice of Lebanon as the new operating base and refuge for his PLO.

The idyll came to an end after Hungary engaged on the losing side in World War I and lost two-thirds of its territory. Capitalist progress depends on the long time horizons of stability and peace. In early 1918, inspired in part by the Leninist Russian Revolution, Hungarian leftists launched two general strikes, followed by the rise of a feckless socialist government amid much carnage. In 1919, a brutal Communist regime took over. Its ruthless poet leader, Béla Kun, a secular Hungarian Jew, cherished a letter of advice from Lenin: "Make these promises to the peasants...Make these pledges to the proletariat...Give these assurances to the bourgeoisie...Do not feel in any way bound by these promises, pledges and assurances."

With Jewish Communist henchmen numbering some 161 out of the top 202 officials in his government, Kun murdered 6,000 "class enemies," focusing on bankers and financiers, many of them Jews, but missed von Neumann's family, which rushed off to a vacation in their summer home and then proceeded to Vienna. Kun's Leninist-certified methods, for all their violence, failed to establish his regime. Within months, a new Fascist leader, Admiral Miklós Horthy—who ruled Hungary during the interwar period from 1920 as well as throughout the Second World War—took over and perpetrated mass murders of his own, punishing Communist Jews while inviting useful bankers such as Max [von] Neumann back to Budapest to revive the economy. But conditions in Hungary had taken an irretrievable dive.

A new law, then unique to Europe, barred all but 5 percent of the slots in universities to Jews. The general turmoil, together with the flight of much of the professional and business class of Hungary, plunged the country into chaos, poverty, and crime. As many tyrants before and after, Horthy attempted to take over the means of production and discovered that they were merely so much iron and dirt without the men of production who made them work. As unemployment soared to more than 30 percent, the chief victims of the Jewish flight were the poor and peasants of these countries.

Von Neumann, though, learned a redemptive lesson about the world. Never would he imagine that wealth and security were stable and predictable. Never would he drop his guard before the evil and treachery of humankind. As he told his friend and colleague Eugene Wigner many years later, "It is just as foolish to complain that people are selfish and treacherous as it is to complain that the magnetic field does not increase unless the electric field has a curl. Both are laws of nature."

Accompanying his tragic sense of history, however, was von Neumann's vision of the hierarchies of knowledge and aspiration. He could climb up from the morass of mittel European politics on the abstract ladders of mathematics and philosophy. As epitomized by von Neumann and Einstein, European Jewish scientists of the time possessed a passionate faith in the coherence of the cosmos. Underlying, suffusing, informing, and structuring the universe, so both believed, is rationality and meaning. In its way, it was a religious faith as formidably fecund as the Jewish monotheism of the Torah from which it ultimately stemmed, and it found its liturgy in the logic of mathematics.

Einstein's greatest attainments, general relativity and the equivalence of energy and mass ($E = mc^2$), were expressions above all of his monotheistic faith that the entire universe epitomized a profound inner consistency and logic, embodied most purely in the aesthetic beauty and wholeness of mathematics.

This faith, the algorithmic faith, ultimately would save the West. When Budapest collapsed into anti-Semitic furies, von Neumann escaped harm mostly through his supreme prowess in mathematics. Introduced by an inspiring teacher, Laszlo Ratz, to the great mathematician Michael Fekete, von Neumann by his senior year in high school already had published a significant original paper on the set theory of Georg Cantor. Above the abstraction of particular numbers themselves, set theory addresses a higher level of abstraction in algebraic symbols of numbers, then moves on up to yet a third level of abstraction: groups of numbers with common logical characteristics. Algorithms on algorithms, their study illuminates issues of the foundations of mathematics.

This set theory paper demonstrated that by the age of fourteen, von Neumann was already delving beyond the superficial craft and processes of mathematics toward the ultimate truths beyond. He then went to Germany to study chemical engineering, for protective coloring in a practical science useful to the Reich, while keeping a position in the embattled PhD program in math in Budapest.

In Germany, von Neumann became a protégé of David Hilbert at the legendary University of Göttingen, a relationship that would shape von Neumann's first great ambition and achievement. Between 1772 and 1788, Joseph Lagrange had translated Isaac Newton's mechanics into coherent mathematics. As Heims explained: "It was von Neumann's deep insight in 1926 that if he was to be the Lagrange of quantum mechanics it would be his task to extend to physics the axiomatic regime Hilbert was imparting to mathematics."

Reaching back to his own previous work in axiomatic set theory, von Neumann succeeded, providing a unified axiomatic foundation for all forms of quantum mechanics, showing how quantum theory reflected a deeper stratum of mathematical logic.

With his childhood friend Eugene Wigner, he elaborated on his insights, writing four important papers extending quantum theory from the simple lines of the hydrogen spectrum pioneered by Niels Bohr to the thousands of lines of more complex atoms. This feat was regarded by atomic physicist Hans Bethe as von Neumann's supreme achievement.

In this pioneering work on quantum theory, as throughout his later career, wherever he operated in the domains of logical systems, von Neumann triumphed in part because of his embrace of Gödel's incompleteness law. Whether in Cantor sets of pure numbers, quantum mechanics, logical systems, pure games, computer science, or information theory, every system, algorithm, computer, or information scheme would depend on assumptions outside its particular system and irreducible to it. Mathematics ultimately would repose on a foundation of faith. As the atheist economist Steven Landsburg puts it: "Mathematics is the only religion that can prove it's a religion." The universe rests on a logical coherence that cannot be proven but to which all thinkers must commit if they are to create.

Early in his life, von Neumann recognized those realms in which science could achieve completeness and where it could not, how logic could be embodied in machines, and what its limits were. These insights into the powers and borders of axiomatic thinking made von Neumann at once the most visionary and the most practical of scientists and leaders.

Von Neumann's contribution to quantum theory was made at the age of twenty-three. He followed a long passage from that moment of intellectual preeminence in physics through a role as protagonist in several other disciplines. In the end, von Neumann's genius was part of a movement of mind that rescued Western civilization from the chaos and violence of his lifetime.

• • •

The decisive event for the Allied victory in World War II sprang from the Manhattan Project. The Manhattan Project produced the bomb that brought Japan to its knees and ended the war. If Germany, Japan, or any of the Axis or Communist powers had been the first to acquire nuclear weapons, the ultimate triumph of the West would have been impossible.

Von Neumann was a major figure in the creation of the bomb. As Kati Marton wrote in *The Great Escape*, a history of Budapest's "Zion on the Danube" and its dissolution, "[von Neumann] enjoyed special status [in the Manhattan Project]. He came and went as he pleased, equally respected by the scientists and the military. When people at Los Alamos heard von Neumann was coming they would line up all their advanced mathematical problems. 'Then, he would arrive,' physicist Ralph Lapp [his Los Alamos roommate] remembered, 'and systematically topple them over.'"

Von Neumann's most direct contribution to the creation of the atomic bomb was to solve "the plutonium problem." Because the separation of fissile uranium-235 from uranium-238 was a slow process performed by hand, this single source could sustain the creation of only one bomb, which no one could be sure would work, or, if it could work, how well, and, finally, whether the Japanese would believe that there was only one such bomb in the Allies' possession. To build more bombs would entail using the more readily-available element plutonium. But no one knew for sure how to trigger a reaction in plutonium. Von Neumann's proposal was an implosive process. Using any available computing equipment to calculate the complex non-linearities, von Neumann ended up specifying the process for unleashing a shock wave optimally shaped to compress a fissile mass. Spurring the project by some twelve months, this breakthrough enabled the team to produce the 60 percent more powerful Nagasaki bomb in time to end the war in the Pacific theater.

The Manhattan Project imposed the essence of the Israel test. Capable of anti-Semitic sneers, particularly toward the mercurial Leó Szilárd, Brigadier General Leslie Groves, in charge of the Manhattan Project, seems an improbable hero in this story. A stiff and conventional military man and a rigid Christian of a sort disdained by intellectuals, Groves represented the "authoritarian personality" that critics of bourgeois capitalism such as Theodor Adorno believed explained the rise of the Nazis in Europe.

As Kati Marton explained, however, "General Groves, a deeply suspicious person, trusted Johnny von Neumann more than he did most of the other scientists and relied on him for advice that went well beyond mathematics and physics to the strategic." Perhaps, as some have speculated, Groves did not regard von Neumann as a Jew. A superb judge of men, however, Groves was alert to genius. In selecting a director for the Manhattan Project, Groves faced a choice between the stolid and conservative Nobel laureate Ernest Lawrence, who was widely favored for the job, and Robert Oppenheimer, with all his Communist associations. In an act that may well have been decisive in the war, Groves chose Oppenheimer. The general explained, "While Lawrence is very bright, he is not a genius...J. Robert Oppenheimer is a real genius...he knows about everything." By relying on Oppenheimer and von Neumann, Groves passed his Israel test. He enabled Los Alamos to assemble in the desert a critical mass of genius and ingenuity that propelled the Manhattan Project to triumph.

As always von Neumann's vantage point was the algorithmic realm, the center of the sphere, from which opportunities open up in all directions. This was also the vantage point of Einstein, who famously refused to contemplate the empirical data until he had deduced and perfected the logical structure of his findings. Neither was religious in any traditional way, but both reflected the Jewish insight of monotheism: a universe ruled by a single mind lending it order and significance.

Heims explains von Neumann's strategy: "It became [von Neumann's] mathematical and scientific style to push the use of formal logic and mathematics to the very limit, even into domains others felt to be beyond their reach" regarding the empirical world, "probably even life and mind, as comprehensible in terms of abstract formal structure."

Bottom-up induction, stemming from empirical measurements alone, occurs not at the center but on the surface of the sphere. Induction requires theories—every experiment entails a concept to guide it—but the theories at the heart of scientific progress are often unacknowledged and mostly undeveloped. This inductive approach has ruled much of late twentieth-century science, driving it to an inexorable instinct for the capillaries. The unacknowledged governing idea is that the smaller an entity, be it particle or string—and the larger and more costly the apparatus needed to conjure it up—the more important the entity is. By rejecting this approach von Neumann left as his greatest legacy the most ubiquitous, powerful, adaptable scientific "apparatus" humanity has ever known—and it made a new world.

• • •

Today, essentially every practical computer in the world is based on the "von Neumann architecture." As early as 1943, he had declared himself "obscenely interested" in computing machines. He soon managed to transmit his obsession to the Manhattan Project, to missile research, to game theory, and to the modeling of economic activity. As he told a friend: "I am thinking about something much more important than bombs. I am thinking about computers." What he was thinking would thrust mankind more deeply than ever before into the algorithmic realm, the computer era, the information age.

A crux of the information age is the law of separation: separation of logic from material substrate, content from conduit, algorithm from machine, genetic message from DNA molecule. In biology, Francis Crick dubbed this proposition the Central Dogma: information can flow from the genetic message to its embodiment in proteins—from word to flesh—but not in the other direction. In communications, any contrary flow of influence, from the physical carrier to the content of the message, is termed noise. The purpose of transmission is to eliminate or transcend it.

The governing scheme of all communication and computational systems is top-down. Applying to everything from the human body to the cosmos, hierarchical systems proceed from creative content through logical structure or algorithm, and then to the physical substrate or material embodiment, which is independent of the higher levels. The von Neumann architecture would be the expression in computer science of this hierarchy and separation.

Just as von Neumann insisted that the axiomatic content of quantum theory be separate from particular physical models, he resolved that his computing machines be independent of vacuum tubes or relays or magnetic domains, or any other material embodiment. He wanted a general-purpose computing machine with a design so scalable and adaptable that it could survive the spiraling advance of the technology.

The crucial step in achieving adaptability was separation. Von Neumann would separate the physical memory from the physical processor and then keep both the data and, crucially, the software instructions in memory, fully abstracted from the "mechanics" of the processor. This separation distinguishes a general-purpose from a special-purpose computer.

A mechanical device physically embodies its algorithm, its "instruction set," in the material form of the machine. But this embodiment makes the one captive to the other: one machine, one algorithm. A vivid example is a classic Swiss watch, a special-purpose computer that achieves its goal only by a fantastically precise mechanical rendering of a single algorithm. If computers were built like Swiss watches—a dead end toward which computer science actually did proceed for a time— each one would be a multimillion-dollar device good for one and only one function.

By separating the memory from the processor, and maintaining the processor's instruction set not in the mechanics of the device but in its fully abstract, algorithmic form as software in memory, a von Neumann machine would be able to perform an infinite number of algorithms or programs, ushering in the computer age.

Von Neumann was the first to see that "in a few years" it would be possible to create computing machines that could operate "a billion times faster" than existing technology. Vindicating his vision, the von Neumann architecture freed the industry from contriving an ever-changing panoply of special-purpose machines and enabled engineers to focus on building speed and capacity in devices, such as memories and microprocessors, whose essential designs have remained unchanged for decades.

The von Neumann machine assumed its first physical form at the Institute for Advanced Study (IAS) in Princeton, to which von Neumann moved in 1930 from the increasingly treacherous politics and parlous economics of Europe. With his mother and his two younger brothers, he had come to the United States after the death of his father in 1929. All around the globe, scientists used the von Neumann architecture, embodied in the IAS computer, as a model for their own machines. Expounded in a major paper he wrote in 1945, the von Neumann architecture provided the basis first for some thirty von Neumann machines following the specific "Princestitute" architecture and then supplied the essential logic for all the computers to come.

After World War II, the advisory committee of the Weizmann Institute in Rehovot, Israel, included both Albert Einstein and John von Neumann. At a meeting in July 1947, the presence of these contending masses in orbit at the pinnacles of their prestige must have palpably distended the geometry of the room.

The two men clashed on the issue of whether the incipient State of Israel could use what at that time was considered to be a giant computer. Its architecture would repeat the von Neumann design, created at the Institute for Advanced Study.

Einstein had long been happy to perform experiments that juggled the entire universe in his head, while calling in associates for any necessary computing assistance. He could see no reason for the tiny embattled agricultural country to acquire a computing machine that could consume 20 percent of the Weizmann Institute's annual budget.

"Who would use it?" he asked. "Who would maintain it?" He implied that the machine was a golden calf in the desert, suitable for worship by miscreant militarists and a distraction from the pure tablets of true science.

Igal Talmi, an Israeli nuclear physicist still at Weizmann, who pioneered a deeper understanding of the "shell" of the nucleus, still remembers the debate. Under Einstein's influence, Talmi made two predictions about the Weizmann Automatic Computer (the WEIZAC.) The first was that "it could never be built because of the limitations of Israeli technology. The second was that if it worked it would be used only an hour a week or so." Talmi was "very happy to be wrong on both points."

John von Neumann, who was not as Olympian or as visionary as Einstein, but was more insightful on such practical matters as building an atomic bomb or a computer, turned out, of course, to be right. To Einstein, he responded that there would be no problem in constructing the machine, or finding uses for it. His former associate at the Institute of Advanced Study, Gerald Estrin, would build the machine and the software engineer and project manager would be von Neumann's own protégé, Chaim Pekeris. Pekeris specialized in such fields as global weather and oceans and interstellar energy patterns that could not be explored experimentally, perhaps even in Einstein's capacious brain.

"Even if no one else goes near the thing, Pekeris will keep it going full time," replied von Neumann.

A tacit undercurrent of this exchange was a dispute between Einstein and von Neumann over whether Israel should develop nuclear weapons. While von Neumann had served in the Manhattan Project and was sure of its virtue, Einstein was wracked with second thoughts and regrets. He called his letter to Franklin D. Roosevelt urging the construction of an atomic bomb "the worst mistake of my life." After the war, he downplayed the Soviet threat and at times believed that the greatest danger to the world was posed by Fascist Argentina and Spain. When McCarthyism erupted in the United States, Einstein at first feared that it could portend a new American fascism echoing Nazi Germany.

As the inventor of game theory, widely used to model arms races, von Neumann understood that a decision by the United States or Israel to forgo nuclear weapons would greatly increase the incentive for all other countries to build them. The smaller the nuclear capability maintained by the United States, the more tempting it would be for enemies to seek nuclear dominance. In a region full of known enemies, Israel without nuclear weapons would not be viable.

In this confrontation of titans, as in other disputes, von Neumann was far more adept at politics and persuasion. He prevailed, and one of the first von Neumann machines in the world was built at Weizmann. The machine soon justified his confidence. The Pekeris team conducted complex non-linear computations that identified and simulated for the first time the amphidromic spot in the Atlantic where the tides so precisely balanced that there was no movement. The team won the Turing Award, often called the Nobel Prize for computing for this formidable global feat of research computation. At the same time, the Weizmann Institute team fatefully began a program of calculations in nuclear fission that would prove crucial to Israel's survival.

Toward the end of his life (he died in 1957) von Neumann was an intellectual leader in the development of the US response to Soviet nuclear weapons and intercontinental missiles. It was von Neumann who shaped the strategy of deterrence, who defined the missile systems that enabled the deterrent, who, with Edward Teller, a Hungarian-born Jewish physicist, championed the movement to build a thermonuclear hydrogen bomb, who made possible American air defense systems based on computers, and who provided the computational resources for the development of small warheads suitable for delivery on the missiles available to the United States. In general, he fostered and framed American weapons and deterrent strategy throughout the tempestuous immediate postwar period.

As a commissioner of the Atomic Energy Commission, as head of countless commissions on ballistic missiles and nuclear weapons for the United States Air Force, US Navy, and the Pentagon, as a research leader at Los Alamos, Aberdeen, and Sandia, as a valued voice at the CIA, as a consultant with the RAND Corporation, TRW, IBM, and other critical defense contractors, von Neumann was a formidable force bringing order and vision to the chaos of programs and military factions in the 1950s, even as the United States seemed to fall behind the Soviet Union in critical capabilities. Virtually the entire panoply of defense of the United States bore the imprint of von Neumann's brilliance.

Admiral Lewis Strauss, chairman of the United States Atomic Energy Commission and long an admirer of von Neumann, told the story of his death of pancreatic cancer at the age of fifty-three in Walter Reed Hospital in Washington, DC—dying, in all likelihood, of his exposure to radiation while observing nuclear tests. "Gathered round his bedside, and attentive to his last words of advice and wisdom, were the Secretary of Defense and his deputies, the Secretaries of the Army, Navy, and Air Force, and all the military Chiefs of Staff....I have never witnessed a more dramatic scene or a more moving tribute to a great intelligence." They all realized, within the aura of his presence, that they were near to the center of the sphere.

After World War II, the most transformative development in science and technology was the emergence of information technology. As

Edward Teller sagely observed, it was information technology—the rise of computer capabilities and their miniaturization on microchips, nearly all following the von Neumann architecture—that saved America's technical leadership during the Cold War when the United States seemed to slip behind even the Soviet Union.

In government-run bureaucracies, swathed in secrecy, riddled with espionage, and paralyzed by pettifoggery and credentialism, US science and technology could not even outperform the equally secret and bureaucratic programs of the Soviet Union. The Soviets developed more powerful bombs and missiles after World War II than did the United States. They launched Sputnik. They built nuclear weapons and exploded a hydrogen bomb.

What saved the United States were not the secret programs of the Pentagon or Los Alamos and other laboratories but the open enterprises of the computer industry. Created by scores of Silicon Valley companies, full of immigrants from Europe, microchips enabled the United States to miniaturize all the control functions in the payloads of their smaller missiles and to create the MIRV (multiple independently targeted reentry vehicles) system that secured the US lead.

Anticipated in part by Einstein, fiber optics and lasers from Corning and Bell Labs gave computers the bandwidth to connect with one another around the globe. The rise of information technology in the United States also revitalized the US economy, yielding the resources necessary to win the Cold War while also endowing an ever-growing population with an expanding array of goods and services based on electronics.

In touting the twentieth century as an era of Jewish science, I am resorting to a heuristic device. With some daunting difficulty and grievous lacunae, one could even write a history that left out Einstein, Bohr, Pauli, von Neumann, Feynman, and all the other great Jewish figures. Rutherford, Planck, Schrödinger, Heisenberg, de Broglie, von Laue, Fermi, Dirac, Tomonaga, and especially Gödel, Turing, and Shannon, all gentiles, played essential roles in the evolution of twentieth-century science and technology. In recent decades, from Silicon Valley to China, Carver Mead of Caltech became a polymathic figure arguably as influential in the science and technology of his own time as von Neumann had been in his.

Science is a collaborative effort. The Jewish contribution, while crucial and vastly out of proportion to the number of Jews in the population, was not self-sufficient or even always paramount. Nonetheless, Jews were especially central to advances in mathematics and algorithms. Once in 1934, David Hilbert, who had brought von Neumann to the great German University of Göttingen, found himself seated at a dinner next to Hitler aide Bernhard Rust. The Nazi education minister turned to Hilbert and asked pleasantly: "How is mathematics in Göttingen, now that it has been freed of the Jewish influence?" Hilbert replied: "Mathematics in Göttingen? There is really none any more."

Von Neumann did not make as significant contributions to quantum theory as Schrödinger, or greater contributions to the atomic bomb than Fermi; neither did he have more important insights into computer science than Turing, nor on information theory than Shannon. Nonetheless, an objective observer must acknowledge that without the constant contributions of Einstein, von Neumann, and their many associates—without what the Nazis insisted was "Jewish science"—there might be a mathematician or two in Göttingen, but "there would not," as Churchill said, "be a free man in Europe."

Twentieth-century science was not a religious competition. But twentieth-century history was engulfed in a war against Jewish scientists and capitalists, and their flight to the West was indispensable to the Western triumph. Von Neumann remains the only figure to bridge all the most critical physical sciences, technologies, and policy decisions of the era. Von Neumann was the unelected avatar and personification of the Jewish triumph and the Israel test.

Now, in an era long after von Neumann's, we face a new Israel test, based on yet another war against wealth and individual genius. Israel is at the forefront of the next generation of technology and on the front lines of a new war against capitalism, Jewish individuality, and genius.

104

Israel is not a peripheral player nor a superficial element of Middle Eastern history and politics. It is at the center of the sphere.

CHAPTER SEVEN

HIDDEN LIGHT

The most precious resource in the world economy is human genius. Let us define it as the ability to devise inventions and enterprises and to create works of art and science that enhance human survival and prosperity. At any one time, genius is embodied in probably fewer than 50,000 individuals, a creative minority that accounts for the majority of human accomplishment and wealth. Cities and nations rise and flourish when they welcome entrepreneurial and technical genius; when they overtax, criminalize, or ostracize their creative minority, they wither.

During the twentieth century, an astounding proportion of geniuses have been Jewish, and the fate of nations from Russia westward has largely reflected how they have treated their Jews. When Jews lived in Vienna and Budapest early in the century, these cities of the Hapsburg Empire were world centers of intellectual activity and economic growth; then the Nazis came to power, the Jews fled or were killed, and growth and culture disappeared with them. When Jews came to New York and Los Angeles, those cities towered over the global economy and culture. When Jews escaped Europe for Los Alamos and, more recently, for Silicon Valley, the world's economy and military balance shifted decisively. Thus many nations have faced a crucial moral test: Will they admire, reward, and emulate a minority that has achieved towering accomplishments? Or will they seethe in resentment and plot its destruction?

Today, an outsized share of the world's genius resides in Israel. Israel has become a center of innovation second in absolute achievement only to the United States, and on a per capita basis dwarfing the contributions of all other nations, America included. How Israel is treated by the rest of the world thus represents a crucial test for human civilization and indeed its survival.

My interest in Israeli innovation began in 1998, when I invited an Israeli physicist named David Medved to speak at the Gilder/Forbes Telecosm conference. Medved described the promise of "free-space optics"—what most of us call "light"—for high-end communications among corporate buildings and campuses. He also spoke of air force experiments in Israel that used the still-higher frequencies and shorter waves of ultraviolet light for battlefield communications. At a time when most of the world's communications, wired and wireless, were migrating to the electromagnetic spectrum, some of the most important explorations of electromagnetic technology, I realized, were taking place in Israel.

Author of a scientific book on scripture, *Hidden Light*, Medved had a polymathic command of the world's physical and spiritual wisdom that he brought to Israel as part of his *aliya*. Nearly a decade after his Telecosm appearance, Medved introduced me to his son Jonathan, a pioneering Israeli venture capitalist. In his offices high over Jerusalem, the younger Medved told me the startling tale of Israel's rapid rise to worldwide preeminence in high technology.

I had long known that many American microchip companies located their laboratories and design centers in Israel. I knew that, in a real sense, much American technology could reasonably bear the label Israel inside. I was familiar with a few prominent Israeli start-up companies, such as "A Better Place," the electric-car company launched by the fashionplate innovator Shai Agassi, which boldly bypassed the entire auto industry in redesigning the automobile from scratch. I had marveled at Gavriel Iddan's company Given Imaging, with its digestible camera in a capsule for endoscopies and colonoscopies.

But what I learned in Jerusalem was that Israel was not only a site for research, outsourcing and the occasional conceptual coup, but also the emerging world leader, outside the United States, in launching new companies and technologies. This tiny embattled country, smaller than most American states, is outperforming European and Asian Goliaths ten to 100 times its physical size. In a watershed moment for the country, in 2007 Israel surpassed Canada as the home of the most foreign companies on the technology-heavy NASDAQ index; it is now launching far more high-tech companies per year than any country in Europe.

To take but one example among many, Israel is a prime source not only of free-space optics but also of another form of hidden light: ultra-wideband. This technology features wireless transmissions that are not, like cell-phone signals, millions of hertz wide at relatively high power, but billions of hertz wide—gigahertz—at power too low to be detected by ordinary antennas. The technology is typically used for mundane purposes, such as connecting personal computers and televisions wirelessly. Israeli companies Amimon and Wisair perform this feat. But a firm called Camero, in Netanya, Israel, has invented an ingenious ultra-wideband device that enables counterterrorist fighters and police to see through walls and identify armed men and other threats within. An easily portable box about the size and weight of a laptop computer, Camero's Xaver 400 could suffuse an urban battlefield with hidden light that would penetrate walls and bunkers and be detectable only by its users. Such inventions are changing the balance of power in urban guerrilla warfare, to the advantage of the civilized and the dismay of the barbarians.

As I investigated companies such as Camero, it became clear to me that Israel had achieved a broader miracle of hidden light illuminating the American and world economies. As late as the mid-1980s, Israel was a basket case, with inflation rates spiking from 400 percent to nearly 1,000 percent by early 1985. As recently as 1990, Israel was a relatively insignificant technology force, aside from a few military initiatives and its perennially inventive agriculture. Yet in little more than a decade, the country had become an engine of global technology progress. Still more important, Israel's technology leadership has made it our most vital ally against a global movement of jihadist terror. How did it make such an astonishing leap?

With the history of twentieth-century science largely a saga of Jewish accomplishment, technological leadership might have seemed foreordained after World War II for the rising Jewish nation. Yet for all the incandescence of deserts in bloom, the miracle did not occur quickly. For many decades after Israel achieved independence in 1948, the Jews who had assembled there generated few significant companies or technologies, no significant financial institutions to fund them, and little important science. Accomplishments made in American states such as California, New York, and even New Jersey exceeded those of Israeli enterprise, and Jews outside Israel far outperformed Jews within Israel.

In the country's early years, its research activities were predominantly public, devoted to defense, and paltry by any standard. As late as 1965, the ratio of research-and-development spending in Israel to its gross domestic product was less than 1 percent, nearly the lowest in the entire Organisation for Economic Co-operation and Development, behind only Italy. Just one-tenth of 1 percent of Israel's employees were engineers, placing it far behind the United States and even Sweden. Michael Porter's definitive 1990 study, *The Competitive Advantage of Nations* mentioned Israel only once.

All this came despite the presence of the Technion University, one of the world's supreme institutions of practical science and the chief contribution of Israel's founders to its eventual preeminence in technology. Located atop a hill overlooking Haifa, the institute sprawls over its spectacular site with a massive maze of concrete institutional architecture as formidable as MIT's: labs, auditoriums, nuclear facilities, giant telescopes, and research monoliths, mostly named for American Jewish philanthropists. But nearly eighty years passed after the Technion's opening in 1924, with Jews around the world forging the science of the age in an intellectual efflorescence unparalleled in human history, without any exceptional contributions coming from Israel.

For much of Israel's short history, the country has been in the grips of reactionary forces, upholding a philosophy of socialist redistribution that could only impede its progress. In 1957, a team of American economic consultants found that Israel's "high labor costs... reflected the high degree of job security... [and] the absence of adequate incentive to or rewards for superior efficiency or performance." This was partly a result, they added, of "virtually complete protection from foreign competition." Two years later, A. J. Meyer of the Harvard Center for Middle Eastern Studies noted "uncertainty in the minds of many [Israeli] industrial producers that theirs is the 'good' occupation or that society really gives them credit—financially and in status—for their efforts." He also cited "welfare state concepts [that] often dictate that incompetent workers stay on payrolls."

Many of Israel's Jews, as the writer Midge Decter described them, "were coming into the country armed with their socialism and their ideologies of labor and a Jewish return to the soil." Imagine it: urban socialists trying to reclaim their past glory and save themselves in a hostile world by returning to the soil in a desert! They created communal experiments—*kibbutzim*—and put intellectuals to work with hoes and shovels, for all the world like a Zionist version of Chairman Mao's Cultural Revolution. Unlike Mao's coercive crucible, the Jewish version was voluntary and it succeeded in agriculture. But the Zionist intellectuals did not want to stop there. In a truly menacing *démarche* of ideological madness, they attempted to abolish the family and private property.

They assigned close to a third of the economy to the ownership of Histadrut, a socialist workers' organization prone to threatening nationwide strikes. Under Histadrut pressure, they instituted minimum wages that stifled employment and propelled inflation. Then they imposed more controls on wages, prices, and rents, making everything costly and scarce.

In a general enthusiasm for public ownership of the means of production and finance, the government through the 1990s owned four major banks, 200 corporations, and much of the land. Israel's taxes rose to a confiscatory 56 percent of total earnings, close to the highest in the world, stifling even those private initiatives that managed to pass through the country's sieves of socialism. Often explained as needed for defense against millions of bellicose Arabs, such tax rates had the contrary effect of eroding the economic base that sustains defense spending. Erecting barriers of bureaucracy, sentiment, and culture, Israeli leaders balked the entrepreneurs and inventors who gathered there, creating a country in its way nearly as inhospitable to Jewish geniuses as the European anti-Semitic regimes they had fled.

Far more welcoming of Jewish and Israeli talent in those days were American companies, particularly Intel. It was an Israeli engineer, Dov Frohman, who in 1971 invented electrically programmable read-only memory (EPROM), a chip-based permanent memory that could retain a personal computer's core programming for "boot-up" even when the power was off. Necessary for distributed personal computers, EPROM would contribute some 80 percent of Intel's profits over the next decade and sustain the company's growth to become the world's leading semiconductor company.

With the help of a company called Xicor, started by Israeli Raffi Klein, EPROM evolved into the flash memories that now dominate the industry. Today, under a series of Israeli companies from Sandisk and M-Systems (now part of Sandisk) to Saifun and Anobit, flash memories are a mainstay of the Israeli microchip industry. These devices lie behind many American miracles of miniaturization, from tiny "thumb drives" to Apple's iPods and iPads to Hewlett-Packard's netbooks.

After leaving Intel in 1974 for a philanthropic sojourn teaching electrical engineering in Ghana, Frohman returned to Israel to establish an Intel design center in Haifa. This laboratory soon conceived the 8088 microprocessor, which was incorporated into the first IBM personal computer. In 1979, also in Haifa, Frohman supervised the development of Intel's first mathematical floating-point coprocessor, which transformed the personal computer into a business-ready machine suitable for IBM's favored market. As a guest in the country, albeit an imposing one, Intel could tap the genius of Jews while bypassing the rules, tolls, and taxes that frustrated many Israeli companies.

Following the success of the Haifa design center, Frohman wanted Intel Israel to establish a semiconductor "fab," or fabrication center, in Jerusalem, together with the necessary chemical and engineering support services. At first he battled Intel executive Andrew Grove—himself a Hungarian Jew who became a legendary figure in Silicon Valley—over the costs of training Israelis to run the fab. But in the end Frohman managed to enlist $60 million in subsidies from the Israeli government and led the project to completion in three and a half years.

By the late 1980s, the Jerusalem fab, Intel's first outside the United States, was producing some 75 percent of the global output of Intel's flagship 386 microprocessor and was gearing up to produce the successor 486 as well. Frohman later persuaded Grove to open production plants in Kiryat Gat in the Negev, Israel's desert. Meanwhile, from Intel's Israeli design centers—by now, there were several—emerged several generations of the Pentium microprocessor, as well as the Centrino low-power processor that integrated Wi-Fi wireless capabilities into portable PCs.

For all the achievements of Israelis working for Intel and other foreign firms, Israel's native technology sector was languishing. Redemption came in unexpected forms. One was a new infusion of genius: nearly a million immigrants, chiefly from the Soviet Union, whom Israel had absorbed in the late 1980s and the 1990s. Impelled by constant harassment from the US government—including Senator Henry "Scoop" Jackson's emancipation amendment, which for a decade was attached to any American legislation of interest to the USSR—the Soviet government finally agreed to a frontal lobotomy of its economy. Under Gorbachev, it released the bulk of the Soviet Jews, who had continued, despite constant oppression, to supply many of the technical skills that kept the USSR afloat as a superpower.

The influx of Soviet Jews into Israel represented a 25 percent increase in the population in ten years, a tsunami of new arrivals that would be the demographic equivalent to the entire population of France migrating to the United States. Essentially barred in the USSR, as earlier in most of Europe, from owning land or businesses, many of these Jews had honed their minds into keen instruments of algorithmic science, engineering, and mathematics. Most had wanted to come to America but were diverted to Israel by an agreement between Israel and the United States. Few knew Hebrew or saw a need for it. At best, they were ambivalent Zionists. But many were ferociously brilliant, fervently anti-Communist, and disdainful of their new country's bizarre commitment to a socialist ethos that punished economic success.

At the same time as the flood of Soviet immigrants, a smaller but seminal wave of Americans arrived in Israel from major US corporations, with knowledge of Silicon Valley and an interest in opportunities in Israel. Among them were GE's Morry Blumenfeld, Tyco's Ed Mlavsky, venture pioneer Alan "Ace" Greenberg, US venturers Yadin Kaufmann and Erel Margalit, biotech pioneer Martin Gerstel, and even an eminent economist, Stanley Fischer of MIT, who became governor of the Bank of Israel. Collectively these newcomers to Israel wielded billions of dollars of available capital, petawatts (a quadrillion watts) of impressive brainpower, a well-honed ability to bypass bureaucratic pettifogs, and an Olympian confidence in their own judgment and capabilities.

Mix the leadership of these dynamic capitalists with a million restive and insurgent former Soviet Jews, and the reaction was economically incandescent. Throw in natural leadership from the irrepressible Natan Sharansky, who had faced down years of abusive solitary confinement in the Gulag, and the impact reverberated through the social and political order as well. Sharansky formed a new conservative political party in Israel to mobilize his former Russian compatriots.

This influx of Russians could not be clamped or channeled, tapered or intimidated into the existing economic framework. As Israeli financier Tal Keinan commented, "they could not all work for Intel." Today, immigrants from the former Soviet Union constitute fully half of Israel's high-tech workers.

Despite the dramatic progress of the 1990s, at the dawn of the new millennium Israel still lacked a financial sector capable of propelling the nation into the globally dominant role it stands poised to fill today. To get there would take one more great reform.

Like the launch of a new technology, the successful allocation of capital is an elegant expression of the law of capitalism (from the Latin word *caput* for head) that mind rules matter. Jews throughout history have excelled in this most intellectual of capitalist endeavors. And yet Israel until recently had virtually no investment houses, deep capital markets, or venture capital. With performance fees barred, hedge funds were essentially illegal. "All my Jewish friends were making their money at Goldman Sachs, while Israel's finance was dominated by a heavily subsidized labor union," recalled Keinan.

In the mid-1980s, Yitzhak Shamir's Likud government, with Benjamin Netanyahu as its ambassador to the United Nations, did cut taxes—increasing the rewards of work and investment by some 30 percent, dramatically boosting economic growth, and reducing inflation. As prime minister in the 1990s, Netanyahu also ushered in dramatic deregulation, along with tax cuts that brought in floods of new revenue. Further spurring local entrepreneurs was the Yozma program in 1993, which waived double taxation on foreign venture-capital investments in Israel and put up a matching fund of $100 million from the government. Demand for the money became so intense that the government hiked the amount and doubled the matching-funds requirement. Nevertheless, throughout the 1990s, most of the money powering Israel's technological ascent came from the Israeli government or from American technology companies. As the millennium dawned, Israel had failed to create a financial-services industry or to wrest control of much of Israel's capital from the hands of Histadrut.

The single greatest force driving the Israelis decisively out of their socialist past into the modern world of finance was the ingenuity of Netanyahu. As finance minister, Netanyahu used Israel's financial crisis of 2003 and 2004, precipitated by the latest campaign of Palestinian terror, as a lever to transform Israel's economy from a largely socialized domain dependent on foreign finance into one of the world's most open and flourishing financial systems. In the process, he created what his occasional advisor Keinan today calls "the greatest opportunity in our lifetimes."

An Israeli supply-sider, Netanyahu faced the adamant opposition of Histadrut and its allies in the Knesset. To overcome the hostility to finance capitalism that had long hobbled the Israeli economy, Netanyahu enlisted vital help from President George W. Bush and his treasury secretary, John Snow. Netanyahu sought a sovereign loan guarantee that would give Israeli bonds the full faith and credit of the United States Treasury, so that despite intifadas and other perils, Israel could issue bonds on the same terms as the world's leading economy. Not wanting the United States to appear a patsy, Snow refused to do the deal without a significant quid pro quo, stipulating that Netanyahu secure from the Knesset a series of major financial reforms.

First, Histadrut, which dominates the pension system in Israel, had to give up its direct line to the Israeli treasury, which had guaranteed it an inflation-adjusted 6 percent annual yield. This special arrangement would be phased out over a period of twenty years. Starting immediately with the first 5 percent of its holdings, Histadrut was required to begin finding other ways to invest its $300 million per month of cash flow. Somehow, a financial industry would have to arise in Israel to handle this huge trove of funds.

A second briar-patch reform demanded by Snow was the immediate privatization of Israel's state-owned industries, reducing the government's majority ownership stakes in these companies from an average of 60 percent to minority ownerships of about 20 percent. Among the privatized ventures were oil refineries, nearly all banks, the Bezeq telephone monopoly, and the national airline, El Al.

The third key reform was the emancipation of the financial-services industry, complete with the full legalization of investment banks, international private equity funds, and performance fees for hedge funds. Eliminated were double taxes not merely on investments in Israel but also on international investment activities by Israelis. The Netanyahu-Snow agenda went into effect on January 1, 2005.

In fewer than twenty-five years—starting from those first modest tax reforms of the mid-1980s—Israel has accomplished the most overwhelming transformation in the history of economics, from a nondescript laggard in the industrial world to a luminous first. Today, on a per capita basis, Israel *far* leads the world in research and technological creativity. Between 1991 and 2000, even before the major reforms of 2005, Israel's annual venture-capital outlays, nearly all private, rose nearly sixty-fold, from $58 million to $3.3 billion; companies launched by Israeli venture funds rose from 100 to 800; and Israel's information-technology revenues rose from $1.6 billion to $12.5 billion. By 1999, Israel ranked second only to the United States in invested private-equity capital as a share of GDP. Furthermore, it led the world in the share of its growth attributable to high-tech ventures: an astonishing 70 percent.

Even a year or two later—while the rest of the world slumped after the millennial telecom and dot-com crash—Israel's venture capitalists strengthened their country's lead in technological enterprise. During the first five years of the twenty-first century, venture capital outlays in Israel rivaled venture capital outlays in all of the United States excepting California, long the world's paramount source of entrepreneurial activity in high technology.

Today, Israel's tech supremacy grows ever greater. A 2008 survey of the world's venture capitalists by Deloitte & Touche showed that in six key fields—telecoms, microchips, software, biopharmaceuticals, medical devices, and clean energy—Israel ranked second only to the United States in technological innovation. Germany, ten times larger, roughly tied Israel. In 2008, Israel produced 483 venture-backed companies with just over $2 billion invested; Germany produced approximately 100 venture-backed companies annually. The rankings registered absolute performance, but adjusted for its population, Israel came in far ahead of all other countries.

Venture capital is the most catalytic force in the world economy of the twenty-first century. In the United States, venture-backed companies produced more than one-fifth of GDP in 2010. Today, American venture capital is flagging in the wake of the financial crisis and such regulatory overreach as the Sarbanes-Oxley law that stifles new public offerings with a toll of some $3 million of mandated accounting costs. Thus the emergence of a comparable venture scene in Israel, linked closely to Silicon Valley, is providential not only for the American economy but also for its military defense (which depends on venture capitalists to finance new technology). Israel's economy steamed through the financial crisis with nary a down quarter and with an ascendant shekel. The rising shekel notably failed to abate an unprecedented export boom (with shipments up some 30 percent in 2010 and 2011) in the face of widespread international calls to boycott Israeli goods.

In the second decade of the twenty-first century, Israel's supremely innovative companies made Israel America's premier economic ally. Israel's creativity now pervades many of the most powerful and popular new technologies, from personal computers to iPads, from the Internet to the emergency room and the operating room.

Consider the Israeli leadership in medical instruments. Dr. Raphael Beyar, Israeli inventor-entrepreneur, rich from the 1996 sale for $200 million of his Instent corporation to Medtronics, was head of Rambam medical center in Haifa from 2006 to 2018. The 4,500-physician institution resides in a sparkling white campus beside a gleaming curve of beach below storied Mount Carmel. Allied to nearby Technion, and to the noted Rapaport Medical Faculty, Dr. Beyar's institution not only provides lifesaving services to more than 100,000 patients annually from around the Middle East but extends its influence to the world through its frequent breakthroughs in medical research and technology.

Among Rambam's accomplishments are two Nobel Prizes and what is said to be the world's most innovative embryonic stem cell project. Its researchers also have produced such companies as Biosense, which has revolutionized the treatment of dangerous cardio-fibrillation. Biosense's catheter is able to capture a 3D voltage map of the heart accurate enough to guide ablation of specific tissue for the cure of arrhythmias.

Medical advances in Israel metastasize to the United States with almost zero delay, saving lives and imparting gains for the US economy. Purchased by Johnson & Johnson for $500 million, Biosense, for example, has become J&J's fastest growing division. Bringing the value of its inventions home to me, two of my brothers are now enjoying the benefits of this treatment for otherwise intractable heart problems.

In the 1980s, Rambam imaging advances transformed the treatment of burns by the use of rapid Computerized Tomography scans, a technique quickly adopted by the US military. After 2000, Rambam's imaging department began an intense collaboration with GE on hybrid medical imagers called CT-SPECT that allow complete appraisal of heart conditions without invasive tests.

A pioneer of stem cell innovations, Rambam also supplied the two most-used embryonic stem cell lines out of five approved by the American National Institutes of Health under the Bush Administration for government supported research in the United States. Bringing unique therapies and technologies to patients from around the globe, this hospital illustrates the centrality of Israel in the global economy of the preservation of human life.

Israel's contributions to American interests do not end with stents and stem cells, catheters and computerized tomography. Spurring the entire US information sector, Israelis continue to supply Intel with many of its advanced microprocessors, from Sandbridge to the Atom. Israeli companies endow Cisco with new core router designs and realtime programmable network processors for its next generation systems, Apple with robust miniaturized solid state memory systems for its iPhones, iPods, and iPads, and Microsoft with critical user interface designs for the OS7 product line and the Kinect gaming motion sensor interface, the fastest rising consumer electronic product in history.

For agriculture and acquaculture, Israeli companies continue to innovate world-leading technologies for water management and desalination. An Israeli company called Beeologics has even invented a remedy for the virus afflicting beehives, which jeopardizes agricultural productivity around the world.

For the US military—among many contributions—Israel provides some 600 upgrades for the F-16 fighter jet, key sensors and algorithms for Predator drones and missiles, and protective equipment for battlefield vehicles. At a time when all the cities of the world are vulnerable to terrorist missile and rocket attacks, and Israel is the target of some sixty thousand missiles near its borders, this tiny country is addressing a central strategic crisis facing the world's civilized nations. It has developed crucial software for the Arrow anti-missile system, for David's Sling against intermediate range attacks, and single chip systems that enable the Iron Dome defense against batteries of nearby rockets.

There is no natural resource or global asset or American ally anywhere in the Middle East—or likely in the world—that compares in value to the genius of the Israeli people.

With a command of information theory, a mastery of the electromagnetic spectrum, and a sophistication in real-time algorithms, Israeli companies are also spearheading the move of the Internet to wireless forms. With Cisco predicting a twenty-six-fold rise in wireless Internet traffic over the next five years, wireless mobility will generate markets as large as the previous wireline Internet era.

Crucial will be a technology called software radio that enables a single device to receive signals from any wireless network (rather than requiring a separate hardwired circuit for each protocol and spectrum band). Under the leadership of CEO Gilad Garon, Israel's ASOCS is the world leader in software radio technology. Originating in large scale electronic warfare and anti-jamming technologies for the battlefield devised by two Russian immigrants, these now one-chip systems can fit in a handset and enable intercommunication among the towers of Babel in urban America.

Israelis also lead in computer chips using parallel processing to sense, accept, and parse information as quickly as modern transmission techniques—especially fiber-optics lines—can deliver it. A representative device in this "fiber-speed" effort, and a powerful symbol of Israel's leading position in Internet technology, is the "network processor." Just as a Pentium microchip is the microprocessor that makes most PCs work, the network processor is the device that makes the next-generation Internet work, doing the vital routing and switching at network nodes. The next-generation Internet will allow "petaflops" (ten to fifteen floating-point operations per second) of real-time computational power to be deployed to virtually any point on the planet. The network processor will let any desktop computer access data and processing power exponentially greater than that incorporated into any PC or any single corporate data center.

The next-generation Internet and its associated technologies will be both the next great machine of capitalism and the next great weapon in its defense. Leading the field are companies such as Eli Fruchter's EZchip (in which I have long been an investor), launched in the late 1990s with a few dollars, no customers, and a compelling PowerPoint presentation in lieu of any actual products. In less than a decade, EZchip drove most of its rivals—firms like Intel, Motorola, and IBM—to the sidelines, and welcomed the rest, like Cisco and Juniper, to its list of major customers. Cisco had previously turned to Israeli innovator Michael Laor to develop two of its core routers that met the explosion of Internet traffic in the late

1990s. Now as the network infrastructure girds to meet a new surge of traffic, Laor is developing a new generation of fiberspeed technology in his own company Compass EOS (ten percent funded by Cisco). Laor's new routers are based on ingenious inventions that channel traffic to and from the machine in optical form at the speed of light. Only at the heart of the router, where new paths are computed and information packets are parsed, does electronics still prevail—in the form of an EZchip. EZchip is becoming the chief source of network processing in the switches and routers of the net.

During a trip to Israel in 2008, Fruchter, Amir Eyal, and Guy Koren of EZchip took me out to dinner in Caesarea. The restaurant was on the Mediterranean beach. Above the beach stood the ruins of Roman temples and terraces, theaters and arches, all recently resurfaced with golden sandstone and carefully refurbished and illuminated. The lights of nearby shops and restaurants glittered along the beach. The rush of the sea on the sand, the scent of grilled fish in the air, the glow of sunset, and the lights on the Roman stone all lent the area a magical feeling of peace and prosperity.

I thought of Gaza, fewer than 100 miles to the south, with similar beaches and balmy weather, and similar possibilities for human advancement. Could the Gazans join the Israelis to create a Riviera on their exquisite beaches, their glowing sands? To do so, they would have to leave behind a world of zero-sum chimeras and fantasies of jihadist revenge. And they would discover that their greatest ally is a man long portrayed as their most feared enemy, a man who, having led for decades the fight to liberate Israeli Jews from self-destructive socialist resentment, now offers to bring all of Palestine and perhaps all of Arabia on the same journey.

The vision of Benjamin Netanyahu is of an Israel that, as a global financial center, could transform the economics of the Middle East. Israel could become a Hong Kong of the desert. Just as Hong Kong ultimately reshaped the Chinese economy in its own image when Deng Xiaoping mimicked its free economy, Israel could become a force for economic liberation in the Middle East, reaching out to Palestinians and other Arabs with the attractions of commercial opportunity. After all, it has long been Israeli enterprise that has attracted Arabs to Palestine.

Netanyahu has long believed that the peace process as we know it is irrelevant, focused on a handful of issues that only serve to breed anger and perpetuate conflict. Meanwhile, true peace—and the promise of a decent life—actually beckons those Palestinians and Israelis who are willing, and now increasingly able, to invest in creation over destruction.

CHAPTER EIGHT

PEACE NOW

Next to the Dan Hotel in Tel Aviv is the glittering Raphael Resto-Bistro, featuring culinary specialties from Morocco and Japan. My host for the evening, Shaul Olmert, oldest son of then-prime minister Ehud Olmert, takes me to a table in the middle facing a panoramic front window.

Named after a novel by the pioneering Zionist Theodor Herzl, Tel Aviv (*Hill of Spring*) is a grand modern city full of the feel and spirit of Silicon Valley's San Jose, with a beach. The Raphael overlooks Tel Aviv's seafront promenade. At sunset, as we sit down for dinner on a December day, a stream of joggers plods by across the sand with the sweaty seriousness of Californians.

Olmert has been a Californian, working in Irvine for MTV Corporation, adapting their TV properties to the digital-game industry. Now he has gone on to become a game-technology entrepreneur himself. As the son of the former prime minister, he saliently represents a new generation of Israelis, perhaps the most entrepreneurial cohort of all, offering new promise for the future of his country, and perhaps a portent of its still possible failure.

The Resto-Bistro chef is the young Olmert's pal and will ply his guests with suitably exotic fare—"don't bother about the menu," he says. "Do you want Israeli wine or Californian?" Then, sampling the best Israeli wines and *hors d'oeuvres*, Shaul will answer a question on the sources of Israeli entrepreneurship by talking about survival.

He recounts the astonishing trek of his grandparents, Mordechai and Bella, escaping with their parents from the pogroms of Odessa in the Ukraine in 1919 across the Russian steppes all the way to China, where they eked out a living in Harbin in the northeast, learned Mandarin, briefly married others before finally decamping to the wilderness of 1930s' Palestine. "They had to give up everything, all their possessions, every convenience, to make it happen," as Shaul puts it. "They were innovators, border crossers, rule breakers, entrepreneurs of survival. They were Zionists above all, but they were citizens of the world. Mordechai's last words were spoken in Mandarin."

He pauses. "Did you like those appetizers?"

"Yeah they're 'licious," I mumble through a mouthful of hummus, salmon, and wasabi.

In Palestine, the saga of the Olmert's grandparents became even more tempestuous. It was not simply entrepreneurship or nimble survival tactics. Mordechai joined the guerrilla group Irgun to fight against British limits on Jewish immigration to Palestine and against what he saw as the appeasement of Britain and the Arabs by David Ben-Gurion's Mapai Party and its military arm, Haganah. Called terrorists at the time and still today, and pursued by Haganah during the "Hunting Season" of 1945, the Irgun under Menachem Begin demonstrated that the British could not pursue their imperial romance with the Arabs without cost. As the Irgun argued, violence was "the new Esperanto" (the once-fashionable "world language" created by the Jewish physician Ludwik Zamenhof).

At a time when Europe's death camps were in full operation, causing Jewish refugees to flee Europe by the millions, and Arabs under the leadership of the British-appointed Grand Mufti Haj Amin al-Husseini were already avid for a new Holocaust, the British were cutting back drastically on immigration to Palestine. Appeasing the Arabs who had allied with the Nazis, rather than rewarding Jews who had fought them, the British were proposing to limit the numbers of Jewish immigrants to Palestine to 75,000 over five years.

In the context of the time, the Irgun was fully understandable and may have played a key role in the formation of the new state. Irgun's most infamous terrorist act, the 1946 bombing of the British Army Headquarters at the King David Hotel, was preceded by three phone calls warning the occupants to evacuate. With the state on the way in 1948, Begin gave up all resistance. Mordechai Olmert, who had first come to Palestine at twenty-two in 1933, and his wife, Bella, lived to see the troubled birth of Israel. In the end, their son Ehud would grow up to become mayor of Jerusalem and then prime minister.

"In Israel," explains young Shaul, "you keep coming up with ways that will allow you to survive and allow you to grow. This is why Israelis are so innovative. We have to be entrepreneurs, to survive."

"But it's not just survival," Olmert continues. "The second reason for Israeli innovation is...Look around you." He waves his arms toward other tables full of diners in denim and suits with faces evocative of a similar scene in San Jose. "You see people that look like Russians, like British, like Iraqis, Ethiopians, different cultures, thrown here together at the same time, with the need to survive. Within three months in the States, you're an American. You feel like an American. But in Israel it's different. There are so many cultures, and no one culture defined Israel before that, so each one of us adopted some of the culture of the other. This leads to tolerance of other cultures and a talent for dealing with them."

After stints of education in new media at the University of Stuttgart and New York University, and employment in London, Los Angeles, Paris, and New York, and even some surfing in Huntington Beach, California, Olmert began thinking globally. He smiles: "When I was in the States, my friends at MTV used to say: 'You go deal with the French people at Vivendi. We really don't get those guys. Those guys are impossible. You go to Paris and work it out.' As an Israeli you are a citizen of the world. You live your life adjusting who you are talking to and who you work with."

Now, as a serial entrepreneur of video-game companies, Shaul claims the world's first system for "streaming applications over the net," the world's first OS-neutral video-game player runtime engine, and the world's first set of in-game utilities to enhance the realism of the experience of massively parallel online multiplayer games such as World of Warcraft ("Look, Mom—no browser!"). The claims are arguable. But here the great challenge of survival is to reach the next level of the game—whether it's "hyperspace" or a NASDAQ IPO.

"Nothing excites Israelis so much as the idea that something is impossible. Goes back to the fact that the whole being of this State of Israel is risky. The entire state is a new venture." As *Fox News* pundit Dan Senor and Saul Singer of the *Jerusalem Post* wrote in their best selling book, Israel is the *Start-Up Nation*.

Olmert goes on: "If you want to send a space ship to Mars...next Thursday...you will get Israeli engineers to work on that project, and the spaceship will go out to Mars next Thursday...but it might not come back.

"If you want the spaceship to go to Mars every Thursday and come back you want American engineers. It will take longer but it will go to Mars every Thursday and it will come back.

"The Americans are good at systems and planning," he observed. "I wish the Israelis were better at planning. But they're not. But they are good at innovating."

Shaul is sure that Israel's test of survival, daily undergone, is the secret of Israeli enterprise. "When you're concerned about your survival, *every day*, you think outside of the box."

As he says this he imagines that he has been doing it, thinking out there beyond the "pale of settlement," beyond the flapping tongues and flags of tradition. But for all his talk of innovation and survival, Shaul is an utterly conventional follower of the Israeli Left.

He is uncertain how his wealth contributes to the world or to Israel. "Wealth is finite," he says. "If one side gets too much, the other side will suffer." As his colleague Itzik Ben-Bassat explains his game technology to me, Shaul looks off into the darker recesses of the restaurant with a look of anxiety, the features of his father imprinted on his handsome young face, but as if haunted by a harrowing memory or a portentous future lurking in the darkness. It seems as if all is not well with the rebel youth and his virtual games, as if from the kitchens of the seaside bistro may burst forth at any moment a Palestinian mob of busboys and waiters demanding a redistribution of the wealth, or an Arab capital in Tel Aviv, or as if his father might suddenly loom up out of the shadows and reproach the son for his globalist views and hedonist games. Shaul wants to move ahead with his company and his life. He is impatient with the perils and moral entanglements of his country. Playing it safe, he retains his apartment in New York and will send his children to summer camp in upstate New York. Like so many, he wants "Peace Now."

"I have never tried to run away from my Judaism," he explains. "As a Jew growing up I heard many stories about the sufferings of Jews, the fear, the Holocaust. As a Jew I'm obliged to be sensitive to the suffering of others. The occupation is making us less moral and less sensitive to the suffering of other people. I don't want to occupy other people. It is important for Americans to be good. I fear that Israelis are losing their moral bearings."

"I want the Palestinians to have a better life," he says.

"The reality today is we're sitting here in this nice restaurant having a nice dinner and an interesting conversation while four million Palestinians live in misery."

"I support the Peace Process and the withdrawal from the territories."

I point out that withdrawal will not help the Palestinian Arabs but betray them to terrorists. As Jonathan Adiri, a top advisor to President Shimon Peres, told us earlier that afternoon, withdrawal is not that simple. I recall standing on a promontory near Gilo in Jerusalem looking down across the valley into the West Bank. We contemplate an elegant four-story mansion a few hundred yards away from which a stream of bullets had issued during the intifada toward an Israeli apartment complex on the top of the hill. Pointing to the entangled weave of ethnic communities, Adiri told us of the failure of all efforts to separate the Palestinian Arabs from the Jews. "We expected the Palestinians to gravitate to their own communities but instead the prosperity and growth in the Jewish parts of Jerusalem acted like a magnet."

From the beginning, the Arabs have been attracted to parts of Palestine that the Jews have been enriching. They don't want to move toward the existing Palestinian communities. They vote with their feet. It is the Palestinians who would benefit from the overthrow of the leaders sacrificing them to the jihad—leaders who say they would rather their people suffer for "a hundred years" than prosper by working with Israelis.

I try a new approach, pointing out that "Arafat died in a house with piles of *Mein Kampf*."

Olmert laughed bitterly and then launched a riff familiar on the Israeli Left: "Yes, I know we did a terrible job in picking our enemies. A lousy job. I apologize. Next time we should do better. We will do better. I promise. We'll audition them better. Find nicer guys to oppose us. I'll give it more thought."

Until then they would seek "Peace Now."

Before meeting him, I already knew that Shaul was not all fun and games. I had read of a petition that he had signed urging Israel's reserve forces to refuse to serve in the "territories." I also learned of his famously lesbian sister Dana, who had joined a rowdy protest march against the Israel Defense Forces for their apparent responsibility for a deadly explosion on a beach in Gaza that accidentally killed eight members of a Palestinian family. "The Intifada Will Prevail," read a placard in the march.

The Olmert family accepted the rebellion of Dana, according to Shaul, and Shaul apologized for embarrassing his father. But they did not recant their positions. As Shaul explained: "My father is paying the price for being a liberal person. It kind of reminds me of this movie *Guess Who's Coming to Dinner?*, this movie in which two parents raised their daughter to be very liberal and very open-minded and one day she comes home from college and brings her new boyfriend and they find out that he's an African American and they are trying to be very liberal and politically correct about it, but they're also kind of stunned by their daughter's choice.

"So I guess that my father was in a similar sort of internal debate throughout our childhood because we definitely used the freedom that we were granted and the encouragement to think for ourselves and develop our own views, and we developed our own views, which happen not to coincide with his."

Nonetheless, the Olmert kids were altogether too trigger-happy in blaming Israel first for violence instigated by enemies set on their country's destruction. In the end, he and his sister are privileged children assuming costly moral postures that are inevitably paid for by the less fortunate. Jihadists will inevitably see pacifism and other dissension in Israel's then "first family" as a sign of weakness. Conspicuous weakness is a prime cause of war.

Olmert reminded me of Bernard Avishai, a similarly impatient Israeli leftist who has published a passionate book entitled *The Hebrew Republic* in a kind of quest for a separate Peace Now. A shaggy professor with a plaintive manner of speech, as I recall from his editing one of my articles for the *Harvard Business Review* some twenty years ago, he has long seen Zionism as "a tragedy." Nothing that has happened in Israel in recent years has dissuaded him from the view that the country as currently constituted is a gigantic mistake. His catalog of complaints echoes Shaul Olmert's: discrimination against Arabs, sorely maldistributed wealth and income, a runaway engine of West Bank settlements that represent an imperial "occupation," and an impending demographic catastrophe caused less by the more procreative Arabs in Israel than by philoprogenitive Haredim and other ultra-Orthodox Jews. Over the last twenty years the Orthodox share of the population has risen from 10 percent to around 25 percent. By any reasonable standard, these defenders of the faith represent the answer to the demographic crunch caused by secular

Israelis with their abortion culture and their gay-rights marches. Yet it is Orthodox population growth that disturbs the Israeli Left.

All in all, in Avishai's vision, Israel is a deeply flawed democracy twisted by special laws favoring Conservative religious Jews and Judaism, by racism and segregation, by the Law of Return, by a labyrinthine separatist wall, by an ethnocentric national anthem and a Davidic flag, and by other grievous offenses to Palestinian Arabs.

In his book, Avishai collects his petitions and amasses his complaints from the usual trio of eminent Israeli writers: Amos Oz, A. B. Yehoshua, and David Grossman. But he adds a variety of Palestinian Arab, Arab Israeli, and Christian Arab vendors of politically blighted belletristic angst, all seeking—with suitable ironic glosses and abraded sensibilities—to blame Israel first for a failure to achieve Peace Now.

The general posture of all these Israeli cosmopolitans is a belief that the conflict in the Mideast is somehow the fault of the Jews, who are too religious and too xenophobic and insufficiently democratic, tolerant, pacific, idealistic, sensitive, sacrificial, and visionary to negotiate a satisfactory peace.

Knowing that, in general, capitalism does not work amid violence, Avishai contends that the prime supporters of Peace Now should be venture capitalists and entrepreneurs. And indeed, like Shaul Olmert, many of them are. Avishai's prime source is none other than Dov Frohman, the inspired inventor and Intel executive whom we have met before. Now he fears that his proud new Intel Fab 18 at Kiryat Gat in the southern Israeli desert will be exposed to attack from the latest generation of rockets in Gaza.

Frohman has long been one of my heroes. He was a pioneering entrepreneur in Israel. But he now lives in the Dolomite mountains in northern Italy for much of the year and has absorbed the syndrome of Euro-pessimism about Israel.

"The vital signs seem okay," Frohman tells Avishai, "but we are really in the dumps, socially, morally, culturally, everything. This is a drugged democracy, which is worse than a dictatorship, because in a dictatorship you try to rebel—and in this place you don't do anything. We need some kind of catalyst to get people to the streets. We need to start talking about social issues—and without the generals doing the talking."

That will do it, I thought. That's just what Israel needs to rev up its economy and impress the jihad: more street protests and more prattle about "social issues."

Frohman is glum even about the technologies he pioneered—which brought me to Israel—and are attracting entrepreneurs and investors from around the world. Told that Bibi Netanyahu deems Israel's increasing lead in technology as a durable basis of national strength, Frohman retorts: "This is bullshit. Bullshit. Investors will not come to us in a big way unless there is political stability... What Bibi says is demagoguery. He's done some of the right things, which in a healthy environment would have been pretty good. But before these policies can have an impact, we'll have more violence."

Frohman disparages the surge of investment in Israel during the first decade of the new century. "There is a lot of financial type of investment but little production type of investment—these are investments which can be taken out at will. And in the meantime, we are losing our reputation as a place for global companies to pioneer."

He asks Avishai: "What will make our entrepreneurs want to stay in Israel, if they don't have quality of life? There is continuous movement of people, they will want to stay elsewhere... But the really critical thing is keeping our young people here. I don't need to do a poll to know that 50 percent of the young people would go."

Frohman and Avishai have absorbed the Peace Now mantra and message that Israel has become an aggressive and even imperialist power. They don't like the Orthodox religious forces in Israel that are the hope of the future demographically, the quarter of the population that bears most of its children. They don't like the politics with its multiple parties and interest groups. They don't like the culture that derided Dana Olmert's gay pride and resisted a planned march of gays, lesbians, bisexuals, transgenders, and multicult singularities down by the Western Wall. They believe that both the gays and the Palestinians are essentially moral and right in their claims. If the Arabs take over Jerusalem, it may become less gay in the Old City, but the Olmerts will be long gone, and Avishai will be tending his garden in Wilmot, New Hampshire. All these Israeli dissidents can justify their multiple-passport lives by echoing the angst of the novelist protestors such as Amos Oz, who puts it as bluntly as any anti-Semite: "We're the Cossacks now, and the Arabs are the victims of the pogroms, yes, every day, every hour."

Is there something about novelists and intellectuals that makes them incapable of grasping the reality of enemies that want to destroy your country and you, enemies contemptuous of all your legal nuances, literary *apercus*, civil-liberties refinements, Booker Prizes, and generous globalist poses? Oz, Grossman, and A. B. ("Bulli") Yehoshua, all proud advocates of Peace Now, all want to give up the land of others—settlers—for what is called "peace."

It has long appeared to be a plausible strategy, upheld by each successive Israeli and US administration and by many sophisticated observers and activist experts blind to the obduracy of Israel's opponents. Israel took land from the Palestinian Arabs in the wars of 1948 and 1967. "Now it is time to relinquish it for peace."

It makes sense. Why not Peace Now? *Shalom Achshav.*

In the end, Shaul and Dana won their debate with their father. Once assertive about Israel's right to settle in Judea, Samaria, and Gaza, Ehud Olmert concluded that because of the demographic trends, Arabs would come to dominate any Israeli state that included the territories. He became the single Israeli prime minister most avidly committed to achieving peace with the Palestinians, Syria, and Lebanon. He supported the withdrawal from Gaza and the removal of some 25,000 Jewish settlers from there. In secret negotiations in 2008 with Mahmoud Abbas, the Palestinian Authority's president, he offered to withdraw from the territories, divide Jerusalem, and give scores of thousands of Palestinians the "right to return" to Israel. He declared the West Bank settlements illegal, attempted to uproot several of them, and was willing to remove all of them, a quarter-million people.

In this pursuit, he gained the support of the Bush administration, which could hardly be more pro-Israel than the Israeli government was. Bush dispatched Secretary of State Condoleezza Rice to the region sixteen times in twenty-one months to bring about peace and to arrange peace talks in Annapolis.

The conventional wisdom is that Olmert, Rice, and Bush were unlucky or maladroit in their negotiating tactics. Experts declared it "ironic" that Olmert, this ardent pursuer of Peace Now, found himself fighting two wars, one in 2006 with Hezbollah, and one in 2008 and 2009 with Hamas in Gaza. Following the withdrawal from Gaza, Israel won no plaudits or support from the international community and no respite from attacks. Since 2001, Hamas and its allies have targeted towns in southern Israel with more than four thousand rockets and thousands of mortar shells. After Israel withdrew entirely from the Gaza Strip in August 2005, rocket attacks increased fivefold.

Following the Hamas rockets came an Israel incursion into Gaza in the last month of 2008 and first month of 2009. Entitled crudely "Operation Cast Lead," it destroyed scores of arms-smuggling tunnels, dozens of ministry buildings and offices, police stations, military targets associated with Hamas, and several Hamas officials.

The result was a huge uproar from the United Nations and other bodies, widespread demands for a cease-fire, and pervasive denunciations of the "disproportionality" of the Israeli response. The *New York Times*, the *Economist*, and *Time* all treated the conflict as an opportunity to tote up the number of claimed civilian casualties on the Gaza side. It was pointed out that the approximately four hundred Gazan civilians lost exceeded by a factor of one hundred the civilian deaths in Israel that provoked the incursion.

When Israel withdrew after twenty-two days amid Hamas's claims of victory, the United States promised some $900 million for Gaza, to be channeled through the United Nations. Since Hamas continued to control Gaza and to intimidate UN officials, who persisted in taking the Hamas side in the conflict, the chances of keeping the money out of Hamas's clutches seemed dim.

In exchange for expending a few million dollars on missiles, the jihadist group (or its Iranian sponsors) would eventually gain three times as much money from the United States ($900 million) as it had reportedly received from Iran. A week later some seventy countries and international organizations convened in the Red Sea resort of Sharm el-Sheikh and pledged an additional $4.48 billion, more than $1.5 billion more than the Gazans had requested. Their cup had indeed runneth over. Again, the donors stressed that the money would all go to the Palestinian Authority, to Fatah rather than Hamas. But Hamas controlled the territory, so it would extort a large proportion of the funds, regardless of contrary intentions. The clear lesson was that terrorism pays and pays. The donors would predictably get what they pay for. So what else is new?

Certainly this sequence of "Peace Now and Then War" was nothing new. It followed the previous even more avid pursuit of the Peace Now agenda by the Clinton administration, when Israel agreed to abandon 95 percent of the territories, financed a new PLO militia to keep order, and committed to a new Palestinian state and a divided Jerusalem. The world was euphoric again, in time with the Nobel Prizes awarded both to Arafat and to Yitzhak Rabin in 1994 for allegedly achieving peace. The result was four years of intifada—suicide bombs and deadly attacks. But this, too, was nothing new.

Similarly, after the 1967 war, in which Israel won a sweeping six-day victory, the country sought peace by proposing to give up its gain of territory. The result was repeated attacks by Nasser's Egyptian army at Suez and then the Arab–Israeli War of 1973, desecrating Israel's holiest day, Yom Kippur. With US support, the Israelis managed to avoid defeat, consolidated their control of Sinai, and established thriving new settlements there. This, too, was nothing new.

Then in 1977, the supposedly bellicose Menachem Begin and the right-wing Likud Party displaced Ben-Gurion's Labor Party in Israel for the first time. The world was appalled. Around the globe and in Israel itself opinion leaders condemned the Israeli voters who, by electing a "former terrorist" to confront the urbane and civilized Egyptian leader Anwar Sadat, had effaced every moral distinction between the Arabs and Israelis. With Begin in power, war was believed to be inevitable.

The result, however, was again "ironic" and "baffling." Peace broke out. Not only did Sadat agree to talks, but he actually traveled to Israel, addressed the Knesset, and aroused the wild acclaim of Israeli crowds. As the wise and courageous Harvard *emerita* professor Ruth Wisse observed in her authoritative book, *Jews and Power*, "The Israeli Hebrew press ran Arabic headlines to welcome the visitor, soccer fans proposed Israeli–Egyptian matches, Israeli radio played Egyptian music. The people of Israel 'fell in love with the enemy.'" Kenneth Levin of the Committee for Accuracy in Middle East Reporting and Analysis (CAMERA) pilloried the phenomenon in his book, *The Oslo Syndrome*, which treats Peace Now as a counterpart of Stockholm syndrome hostages who become infatuated with their captors.

In the Camp David negotiations that followed, the reputedly pugnacious Begin succumbed to the Peace Now spirit. Under pressure from Sadat and then US president and peace paladin Jimmy Carter, Begin gave up the Sinai and expelled the Jewish settlers. Israel might permit 15 percent of its population to be Arab, but the newly friendly Egyptians stopped well short of allowing a small but prosperous Jewish presence on their territory.

In conversation with Sadat, the former Israeli Prime Minister Golda Meir epitomized the Jewish stance, subordinating the pain of loss of Israeli soldiers to the pain of inflicting military losses: "We can forgive you for killing our sons, but we will never forgive you for making us kill yours." It's nice rhetoric, but in the usual liberal stance, she was elevating her own moral feelings above the practical effects of her actions.

As Wisse writes, "This point had been made long before by the foremost exegete Rashi...in his commentary on the passage of Genesis 32:4...'Jacob was very afraid and he was greatly distressed...lest he be killed by his brother Esau, but he was even more 'distressed' that in self-defense, he might have to kill Esau...' Whereas Rashi was expounding this high moral principle for his Jewish audience, Golda Meir was admitting it to an antagonist whose political traditions interpreted her confession as weakness....

"Four years earlier, when Golda Meir had been prime minister, [Sadat] had coordinated with Syria the attack on Yom Kippur....If he now came to Jerusalem to regain the territories lost by Egypt, it was not out of regret for having killed too many Jews but with the realization that he could not kill enough to defeat them."

Even so, his treaty with Israel, however favorable to his country, outraged the Arab League, which maintains a genocidal posture against Israel as its *raison d'être*. The league moved its headquarters out of Cairo to Tunis. Its hostility to Sadat continued until his assassination two years later by Hamas precursors from the Muslim Brotherhood.

But this was nothing new. When King Abdullah of Jordan expressed his willingness to negotiate a treaty with Israel in 1951, he was assassinated by family members of the Grand Mufti of Jerusalem, Haj Amin al-Husseini, at the entrance of the al-Aqsa Mosque in the Holy City. That ended Jordanian moves for Peace Now. And this, too, was nothing new.

CHAPTER NINE

GAMES OF WAR AND HOLINESS

Robert Aumann, a Nobel laureate economist, fled Frankfurt with his parents in 1938 just two weeks before *Kristallnacht*. A wealthy textile tycoon, the elder Aumann, an Orthodox Jew, left everything behind in his flight to New York and, newly impoverished, had to scrounge for work. His son gained a clear notion from his father of the fragility of wealth and power.

Having earned his doctorate in mathematics at the age of twenty-five at the Massachusetts Institute of Technology, he became one of the founders of the Center for the Study of Rationality at Hebrew University, which is perched on Mount Scopus overlooking Jerusalem, and affords glimpses on good days of the mountains of Jordan and the Dead Sea. In 1999, Aumann became the founder and first president of the Game Theory Society. He has taught at Stanford, Princeton, the State University of New York at Stony Brook, Berkeley, New York University, and at the Catholic University of Leuven in Belgium. He gains his insights as the leading living practitioner of the most austere and abstract of sciences: the game theory excogitated in a great synoptic burst by John von Neumann.

Originally based on simple games of strategy, such as poker, it applies to all situations of conflict and cooperation. After conceiving this discipline in a 1928 paper introducing the "Theory of Games," von Neumann developed its full mathematical foundations in stolen moments of collaboration with Oskar Morgenstern during World War II. Their masterpiece, *The Theory of Games and Economic Behavior*, published in 1944 by Princeton University Press, bristles with complex mathematics. Although it was one of the best-received books of the epoch, scrupulously weighed and fathomed by several current or future Nobel laureates among fifteen other major figures in economics and mathematics, it remained too formidable a restructuring of economics from the bottom up and too practical an application of pure mathematics from the top down to be readily absorbed by either of discipline. It caught on chiefly at the RAND Corporation, which was devoted to developing military strategies of nuclear deterrence after World War II.

Von Neumann was acting to save the social sciences from their towers of Babel—macro- and microeconomics, sociology and psychology, evolutionary biology and computer science, business strategy and military strategy, neuroscience and behavioral science, arms races and peace studies—and to unify them all under a single logical theory of rational interactions among purposeful agents.

Seeking to establish the discipline on a coherent mathematical basis, von Neumann and Morgenstern took the study beyond zero-sum games, in which the winnings and losses of all parties added up to zero, to positive-sum games in which profits were generated and winnings exceeded losses. This advance was critical. In zero-sum games, any winnings by an opponent came at the cost of other players. It replicated the law of the jungle and tended to degenerate to the war of all against all. The challenge was how to convert such predatory games from positive-sum games into corollaries of the golden rule, according to which the good fortune of others was also your own.

Von Neumann was always concerned with the dynamics of competitive processes and saw that economic systems could not achieve equilibrium outside an environment of growth. Capitalism is, by nature, a positive-sum game, in which every transaction theoretically can yield two or more winners. As long as the exchanges are voluntary, they will not occur unless both parties believe they will gain from them. This belief may sometimes be wrong. But since winnings accrue to those who arrange good deals for themselves and others, making them the dominant players in the game, the total of winnings—the economy—expands. Thus even less-skilled players also benefit, unless they opt out of the game by behaving in perverse and destructive ways. Shaul Olmert's theory of the global economy as a zero-sum game would have struck von Neumann as silly.

In politics, however, zero-sum outcomes do tend to prevail, with players competing for a limited number of countries, legislative seats, and positions of authority in a finite planetary land mass. A longtime student of Morgenstern and an admirer of von Neumann (whom he never met), Aumann built new and more robust bridges between the zero-sum predicament and the positive-sum world, taking the theory of games to a new level that casts unique light on the predicament of Israel.

Expounding his theory most relevantly and accessibly in "War and Peace," his Nobel lecture in Stockholm in December 2005, Aumann began by drawing a clear distinction between one-time games and repetitive games. He argued that if you are not going to have any future relationships or transactions, a predatory policy is rational. The mugger or terrorist can be a rational man. The pursuer of a one-night stand has no reason not to lie and no incentive to gratify his prey. This grim fact is backed up by a large body of human experience as well as game-theory mathematics.

It is repetition that makes cooperation achievable even when it cannot be summoned in one short game. Repetition of transactions over time and the extension of contracts through time is the heart of capitalism and of peaceful relationships among nations. Repetition is the bridge linking the predatory present, the zero-sum moment, and the long-term sums of mutual learning and wealth.

In order to transform a zero-sum immediate game into a long-term economy, however, the long-term player must penalize bad behavior.

If the predator gets away with his taking, he will continue to take. He will learn the law of the jungle. It is punishment that teaches him the greater gains of mutuality, investment, and trading.

The lesson for Israel is clear. "If you want peace now," Aumann says, "you may well never get peace. But if you have time—if you can wait—that changes the whole picture; then you may get peace now. This is one of the paradoxical, upside-down insights of game theory...Wanting peace now may cause you never to get it—not now, and not in the future. But if you can wait, maybe you will get it now." And Israel can wait. Even the intifada did not interrupt the technology boom, while unilateralism in policy has worked very well.

Aumann's message is that civilization depends on long-term horizons in repetitive transactions. In a single exchange, the rational policy is to be predatory. If predatory actions bring success, a player is never induced to extend the time horizon. By accommodating aggression, a nation invites it. Peace requires the imposition of penalties on aggression.

From his point of view, the pattern of peace initiatives followed by war is neither "ironic" nor "baffling," nor does it suggest that Israel has somehow failed to seek peace with sufficient ardor and resourcefulness. It shows that by relentlessly seeking Peace Now, Israel has predictably and clearly communicated to the Arabs that terror and aggression work. By repeatedly informing the Arabs that it wants peace more than it wants victory, or even territory, Israel evinces a short-term strategy that powerfully and consistently rewards bad behavior. As a result, Israel gets neither peace nor victory, and the Palestinians get neither economic growth nor political progress. Peace Now is essentially a pursuit that gratifies its preening pursuers who believe in their own moral superiority and harrows everyone else.

A critical element in all games is the discount rate, which determines the time value of the reward, the terms on which one can trade benefits now for benefits over the long run. In economics, this factor is quantified as the rate of interest.

Capitalism works because of its long time horizons and low discount rates that optimize cooperative behavior. The time element is crucial to the deepening of capital and the generation of positive-sum games.

The more the players focus on politics rather than on economics, the more the game tends to deteriorate. Without capitalism, democracy is a zero-sum game and leads to conflict and war. Without the increasing economic rewards of an expanding pie of goods and assets, the democratic struggle for power hardly differs from a series of coups. In both cases, the losers are deprived not merely of political power but also of their livelihoods and their futures. The way to transcend the zero-sum trap into the golden-rule economy is to move from political and military relationships to the spirals of gain in capitalist economic interplay. When a "successful" "peace process" must be concluded within the limited four- or even eight-year term of an American president, the instructive benefits of a slow, long-term educational process are lost.

Missing a critical point, as well, are Utopian free marketeers, who imagine that a mere complex of free-trade agreements will bring about a world perfectly pacified by the lures of commerce. Essential to the transition is military power sufficient to defend against any feasible threat. Weakness enhances the rewards of adversaries' military strength. The kind of disarmament sought in the Peace Now movement invariably leads to war because it renders military strength relatively more rewarding than the saving and sacrifice needed for economic advance. Complete disarmament is the most dangerous condition of all because it offers the maximum reward for secret armament. Thus, disarmament is likely to cause the rapid and unpredictable acquisition of weapons and result in imbalances whenever aggression is rewarded. As the US nuclear deterrent deteriorates, for example, the value of the nuclear capabilities in Iran or other hostile countries rises inexorably.

Crucial to successful negotiation is long-term commitment. Irrational behavior may be rational in a game if it conveys an absolute commitment to a goal. An example cited by Aumann is what he brilliantly calls the "blackmailer's paradox."

Alice and Bob must divide a thousand dollars. It is not an ultimatum game; they can discuss it freely. Bob says to Alice, "Look, I want nine hundred of those thousand dollars. Take it or leave it. I will not walk out of this room with less than nine hundred dollars." Alice says, "Come on. That's crazy. We have a thousand dollars. We should divide it evenly."

"You may say it's crazy or not crazy, but I'm not walking out with less than 900." Bob stands his ground, and since 100 is better than nothing, Alice takes the hundred.

The paradox is that the irrational guy is Bob. He is crazy. But he gets the 900 dollars. It would seem that in a rational game the irrational guy should get less rather than more. The answer to the paradox is that Alice can also declare that she's not walking out with less than 900 dollars. Then it becomes a test of wills and capabilities. The important thing is that the person who is making this demand has to convince the other one that he is absolutely serious.

Bob, when he says 900 dollars, has to convince Alice that he is really serious. He's crazy, but crazy and serious are not mutually exclusive categories. Alice, likewise—if she doesn't want to capitulate—has to convince Bob that she, too, is serious. In order to convince the other person, you must first convince yourself. That is another part of the paradox. Conviction is a process of conversion in which identity itself is engaged. Such immovable convictions are often termed religious. In some sense, they transcend reason and partake of the domains of faith. The rational man at some point has to make a religious stand. He makes a commitment by declaring some entity as holy.

All the usual trite objections that game theory is valid only in a world of rational calculators engaged solely by materially calculable goals—economic players—ignore the essential importance of sacred commitments. Focusing on behavior and response, the theory implicitly comprises all motives, including sin and hate, love and worship. If the Palestinians, goaded by more than a century of anti-Semitic propaganda, and mixed with their present-day shame and envy, do in truth prefer killing Jews to life itself or to giving life to a Palestinian nation, then the game will accommodate that motive. Israel will ultimately build a fortress, backed by a nuclear deterrent and any additional combination of deadly or defensive technologies. Precisely by taking the Palestinians at their word, the Israelis may cause them to think again. Perhaps life excluded from the wealthy fortress next door will not be so attractive. Perhaps peace would at last seem preferable.

In December 2008, I traveled to Toronto to hear the seventy-eight-year-old Aumann speak. It was a rare experience of the religion of rationality.

Aumann stood at the podium like a prophet, his long, white beard making him look like the Talmudic scholar he is or like a prophet of yore, his hoary voice tinged with hints of Hebrew, all lending a hallowed resonance to his words, which came slowly, one at a time, as if extracted painfully and precariously from an aging brain, still lagging seven hours, or perhaps thirty-six centuries, behind the times of modern Toronto. For Aumann was trying to explain his ardent belief that his Canadian hosts for the evening, celebrating "Israel at Sixty"—and indeed most observers of Israel and its predicament—had gotten it wrong, very wrong, wrong by many orders of magnitude.

As a preeminent living Israeli scientist and leading exponent of mathematical rationality, Aumann is one of the world's most modern thinkers. Although his prime field is game theory, he is one of the world's leading mathematicians and economists. But his audience that evening was a crowd of politically conservative Jews gathered in the comfort of the synagogue conference center of Aish HaTorah, meaning "Fire of the Torah." In the continuing conflict between the times and the Torah lies a revealing dimension of the Israel test. To the fire of the Torah, Aumann brings the ice of reason, but as the audience would learn, there is enormous fire in his ice.

Nervous about Aumann's initial, halting delivery and long, pregnant silences, some in his audience began shifting in their seats, half fearing that this crusty old scholar might break down. Others worried that he was coming down from his distant mountain in Jerusalem, inflamed with a vision of truth, to deliver an Israel test as a list of mathematical problems. Or that he would unveil a series of stone tablets inscribed with a set of abstruse equations, together with the claim that his listeners must turn from the golden calves of commerce, the Kosher feasts on the groaning boards of this gala event, and the numinous laws of the Torah upheld in this Orthodox synagogue, and bow to the revelation of mathematical logic. But Aumann had something else on his mind that evening. He would explain that his game-theory insights were all of a unity with his monotheistic Judaism. But his first observation was simple, factual, mathematical, and holy.

"Israel," he said, "is not sixty years old. It is sixty times sixty years old."

Gathered to celebrate and discuss "the state of our future" in black ties and evening best, the audience was somber. Earlier in the evening Caroline Glick, then the eloquent Cassandra of The Jerusalem Post, warned the group over dinner of the portentous meaning of the massacre of Jews a few days before at Mumbai's Chabad House in India, where jihadist terrorists took time off from an assault on the Taj Mahal Palace and Tower hotel and other monumental structures inherited from a long-gone empire to torture and kill a small assemblage of Jews at a non-descript school for orphans nearly a mile away.

"They did it," she said, "with long advanced planning and with an ecstatic relish of murderous hatred."

For twenty-four hours, The New York Times, CNN, and other notable media, as she reminded the audience, ignored the attack on the Chabad House. Then in subsequent days they appeared baffled by this digression in the path of terror, which struck the eminent editors of the Times as "senseless." They ruminated on the possible strategic significance of the Jewish center as a vantage point for an attack on Mumbai's more consequential targets, such as military bases or business centers. But Glick readily decoded the message from the bloody rubble and easily read the miasmic minds of the murderers.

"We recognize that wherever we are, the primary target is always us. The essential take-home lesson from Mumbai, the historic lesson from Mumbai, is that we are on our own. Our destiny is in no one's hands but our own. Our greatest achievements have come when we recognized that we must trust in ourselves. The greatest calamities come when we trust in others to save us...

"That is what it means to be free. To look inside ourselves and find what is valuable and good in ourselves and what must be defended. Depending on others is a form of slavery. It is self-awareness of worth and valor that separates a free person from a slave."

Glick's vision prepared the way for Aumann, who continued the lesson.

He began by reading the title of the conference from the program— "Israel at Sixty"—and then he told a story from scripture:

"Jacob and the man, the angel, struggled until the morning came and the man saw that he could not overcome Jacob, though he touched his rib and the rib moved. It was injured.

"The man said 'Send me away, the morning has come, make a truce with me, give me a cease-fire.' And Jacob responded: 'I will not send you away. I will not send you away, until you make peace with me...until you have blessed me.'

"And the angel asked him, 'What is your name?' and he said, 'Jacob.'"

"And the angel said, 'No longer will you be called Jacob, but Israel.'

"That was three thousand six hundred years ago. Israel. Why? Because you have struggled with angels and with peoples and you have been victorious. You made it. And he blessed him.

"Ladies and gentlemen," Aumann continued, "This is what is going on today. These verses reach down through the millennia. Jacob was left alone surrounded by enemies and then a man came and struggled with him. Who was that man? The spirit of Esau. The spirit of the nations, the spirit of the ages. That was the angel who struggled with Jacob. Jacob struggled not with a physical human being but with a conception: anti-Semitism. Beating down the Jews. He struggled with it. He does not give up. He is wounded. But he does not stop. Finally the angel said, 'I have to go.' Cease-fire. Let's make a truce. Let's go.

"'No,' responded Jacob, 'I will not stop until you accept me. You have to make peace with me. You have to bless me.'

"Then the angel said, 'OK, I bless you. Why do I bless you? Why do I make peace with you? Because you have held out in the struggle. You have shown to me you will not collapse. You are holding on to your principles. I have become finally convinced that you are not going to let go. You have convinced me of that. You will not let go. You have struggled with the concept, the idea of Esau, and with physical human beings, and you have overcome both on the spiritual plane and on the physical plane.'

"That is when Israel was created. It was three thousand six hundred years ago. Sixty times sixty years ago. Not sixty years ago.

"So it was up to Jacob. It was up to him and he did it. Just as in Caroline Glick's beautiful remarks at dinner, it's now up to us and we must do it. We have to keep on. If we want the blessing of our cousins, not only of our cousins, but if we want the blessing of the world, we have to keep up the struggle. Although we are wounded. In spite of our wounds. Which we have suffered again and again throughout this struggle, throughout this long night. This is what we have to do. If we want their blessing we have to keep up the struggle from our side."

Then, in the question and answer period, apparently in order to shake up his audience for a learning moment, he insisted, "The terrorists are rational. They are giving their lives. They are heroes of their people. They are heroes...."

The moderator, Adrienne Gold, a Canadian television personality, had had enough of this. She interrupted: "You mean there is no objective rationality? It's all relative?"

"Yes," he proclaimed, "Of course there is no objective rationality. Congratulations. You have got it right. Rationality is the effective pursuit of your goals. The suicide bombers are rational, and they are getting their way. We have to understand they are rational in order to fight them."

"All right. But there is an objective morality. You don't deny that."

"Oh, now you are talking morality." Aumann said. "Morality is something else."

Morality perhaps is the rationality of the law. Or the rationality of the universe.

"For example, morality," Aumann said, "dictates not evicting people from their homes. Ever.

"Over history," he observed, "many peoples have been expelled from their homes. But never before have they expelled themselves. Only the Jews have been expelling themselves, their own people, from their own homes and synagogues, towns and farms. From Sinai, from Gaza, from the West Bank, from Jerusalem. Only the Jews....

"Ladies and gentlemen," he concluded, "if we want to survive as a nation in Israel, we have to go back to Jewish values. There is no other way. We have to reclaim our belief in the holiness of our cause.

"The State of Israel was founded by the Jewish people sixty years ago. It was founded by and large by people who were not observant, [Chaim] Weizmann, Ben-Gurion, Moshe Dayan, Abba Eban, Golda Meir, people like this, and people who came before them. What these people did not realize is that Jewish values do not pass on automatically from generation to generation. They still had the vision. Their children didn't. Or if some of their children had it, their grandchildren did not.

"In Israel, in general, we do not have it any more, not just the political leadership, the intellectuals, the media, the universities, the courts, these people have lost the *raison d'être* of this state. They have forgotten that it is not sixty years old; it is sixty times sixty years old. They have forgotten the struggle of Jacob with the angel. And so the whole thing comes apart in their hands."

Here Aumann entered into the realms of game theory: "What has happened is that nothing to us is holy any more."

Unifying his two visions of rationality and religion, Aumann believes that a vision of holiness is critical to a game's theoretic grasp of Israel's predicament.

He tells a story.

"About eighteen years ago, the last time there were serious discussions between Syria and Israel about some kind of understanding between the two countries, a high officer in Israel, a major general, came by my office in the Center for the Study of Rationality. Why do we call it the Center for Rationality? It's the only place in Israel where there is any rationality at all. It's on the second floor of the Feldman Building on the Givat-Ram campus of Hebrew University in Jerusalem. That's where it is.

"The general came to me and identified himself by his first name. He discussed the situation with Syria. Said if we are going to reach any accommodation with the Syrians, we are going to have to give up all the Golan Heights. We will have to expel all the Jews who have been living in the Golan Heights for forty years. They're going to have to leave the synagogues, leave [northern Galilee], which was one of the last bastions of the Jewish people in Israel at the time of the revolt against the Romans. We are going to have to leave all that, all the homes, all the farms, all the culture. Have to expel all the Jews.

"'Why?' I asked. 'Why can't you compromise with them? Why?'"

He said to me: "Because to the Syrians the land is holy."

I answered: "That's the trouble with us. Not only is the land holy to the Syrians, but they have managed to convince you that it is not holy to us. Nothing is holy to us. Not the Golan Heights, not Jerusalem. Not Tel Aviv. Nothing is holy to us. We do not have any red lines. Nothing at all. And because nothing is holy to us, we are going to be left nothing if we continue this way."

These echoes from the Torah and the primal religious predicament of the Jews might seem anomalous from a man who was awarded the

Nobel Prize for advances in a science invented by the very secular and eminently pragmatic titan von Neumann, a science that attempts to reduce to mathematical logic all the strategic interactions of human beings, from poker and chess to love and religion to naval maneuvers and nuclear war. It is a way, in the words of the late polymathic strategic thinker Herman Kahn, to "think about the unthinkable," to extract the emotion and blood from scenes like Masada and Mumbai, Nagasaki and 9/11, and to arrive at purely rational rules and predictions that render these eruptions more manageable and amenable to mitigation, remedy, or deterrence.

Three years earlier, Aumann concluded his Nobel lecture with a comment on Isaiah: "When Isaiah speaks of lions lying down with lambs and nations beating their swords into plowshares and their spears into pruning hooks and nations learning war no more, he is describing what can happen when a central government prevails—in the presence of a Lord recognized by all. . .

"In the absence of such a dominant hierarchical power, one can perhaps have peace—no nation lifting up its sword against another. But the swords must continue to be there—they cannot be beaten into plowshares—and the nations must continue to learn war, in order not to fight."

This recognition is indispensable to the survival of Israel—and of the United States.

CHAPTER TEN

THE CENTRAL IMPORTANCE OF BENJAMIN NETANYAHU

Both in the United States and in Israel, the first decades of the twenty-first century ended with political change that brought the Israel Test to the fore as the crucial conflict and major line of division in international affairs.

The United States elected Barack Obama, a charismatic exponent of Peace Now, tribune of nuclear disarmament, fervent protagonist of the economics of envy, a tireless and empathetic spokesman for Third World misery and Muslim grievances, and a prominent believer in the idea that among the greatest threats to the world is the impending increase of a couple of hundred parts per million (0.02 percent) in the accumulation of carbon dioxide in the atmosphere. Under the influence of his community-activist mentor Saul Alinsky, Obama brings an unusual anti-capitalist perspective to the Oval Office, unique in its history.

One of Obama's first acts as president was to remove from the Oval Office a bust of Winston Churchill, sculpted by Sir Jacob Epstein and loaned to President George W. Bush by British Prime Minister Tony Blair on behalf of the British people after 9/11. To the new American president, it is safe to assume, Churchill represents a retrograde imperial figure sullied by his support for the British occupation of the Obama family's ancestral domains in Kenya.

Supported by 78 percent of American Jews, Obama's election was a disaster for Israel redeemed only by the subsequent election of Benjamin Netanyahu in Israel. Like his predecessor, Bill Clinton, Obama was a lawyer who saw the world as a Churchillian struggle between good and evil only in the pinched and narrow confines of legal rights and torts, territorial claims and counterclaims, all ripe for negotiation and compromise. He was also afflicted with a Messianic view of himself as a charming and reasonable fellow who could seduce a cobra such as Mahmoud Ahmadinejad into the arms of Peace Now. All his Middle East foreign policy advisors—Hillary Clinton, Samantha Power, George Mitchell, Dennis Ross, Susan Rice, Brent Scowcroft, *et al.*—believe in Palestinian statehood based on an Israeli amputation of "land for peace." In this regard these advisors were utterly conventional, inidistinguishable—indeed admired by—the self-flagellating Jews in Peace Now and J Street movements, as well as the American leftist intelligentsia within the media and academia. Not confined to Democrats, this deluded cohort included the eminent Condoleezza Rice, who ended her stint as secretary of state under George W. Bush as an avid advocate of appeasement. The chief public defenders of Israeli resistance to gouges in Golan and Gaza and jettisons of Judea and Samaria were unfashionable but inconveniently pithy and popular gentile figures such as Sarah Palin, who displayed an Israeli flag in her office in Juneau; Thomas Sowell, in his lucid and visionary columns; Ann Coulter, in her defiant realism; Rush Limbaugh, in his daily radio broadcasts; George Will in his eloquent and incisive reports; and the magnificent orator, the Christian evangelical preacher, John Hagee, founder of the ten-million-strong Christians United For Israel (CUFI.)

Obama's election victory with nearly 53 percent of the vote and a Democratic sweep of Congress unleashed a resolute drive to create a Palestinian state in exchange for the massive security barrier of legal documents between Israel and its murderous enemies.

While the United States moved toward the Left and the Peace Now legalism, Israel veered toward the Right and militant self-defense. Its prime minister, Benjamin ("Bibi") Netanyahu, was the obverse of Obama in nearly every imaginable respect. Although his party won a smaller number of Knesset seats than his opponents combined, an additional fifteen slots were taken by Bibi's former chief of staff and intimate associate Avigdor ("Yvette") Lieberman. These seats gave the right-wing parties nearly the same percent—54 percent, in Israel's case—won by Obama. Running to the right of the newly statesmanlike and circumspect Netanyahu, Lieberman exploited widespread Israeli indignation at visible Arab–Israeli support for Hamas during the 2008 war in Gaza. He received, and perhaps even deserved, bad press for his demagoguery, but he was a rational man with whom Bibi had frequently worked in the past. In any case, under Netanyahu, Israel's leadership offered a striking and instructive contrast with America's.

While the youthful Obama was a community-action organizer and sometime lawyer, who steered clear of any military service, Netanyahu was an anti-terrorist warrior. While Obama imagined that taxes in general were too low and inadequately progressive, Netanyahu was a sophisticated supply-side economist who believed that lower rates brought higher revenues and who opened his administration by advocating tax cuts. While in the past the United States had long offered a haven for frustrated Israeli entrepreneurs and other Jewish capitalists, Israel under Netanyahu would beckon as a land of hope and hospitality to frustrated American venture capitalists and entrepreneurs. While Obama believed that foreign aid was the answer to Palestinian poverty, Netanyahu knew that new opportunities opened up by Israeli enterprise were the only solution to the regional crisis.

While Obama believed that the United States had overreacted to the threat of terrorism, Netanyahu for more than forty years had championed and explained the war on terror in both the United States and Israel, in books, international meetings, and through the Jonathan Institute (named for his late older brother who died at thirty in the stunning Entebbe hostage rescue in Uganda). Netanyahu saw jihad as the single greatest threat to the West, and no other politician was so learned or so determined in combating it. While Obama thought Churchill was a man whose time had passed, Netanyahu had read and pondered all of Churchill's works and admired the British titan "above all other gentiles." The time for Churchillian leadership, according to Netanyahu, was now. His 2015 speech to the American Congress included clear echoes of Churchill's great address to the Canadian Parliament in 1942.

Netanyahu offers far more than an ideological counterpoint to American liberalism. His life story and family legacy make his election a potential historic turning point in the relationship between the United States and Israel. President Donald Trump recognized this, although neither his predecessor nor his successor did, making it clear that Netanyahu was not welcome at the White House. Netanyahu is at once the most profoundly Zionist and the most deeply American of all Israeli leaders, having been educated in the United States as a child and in his undergraduate studies in architecture at MIT and earning his master's degree at the MIT Sloan School of Management. His American English is flawless. In the increasingly global economy, facing an ascendant jihad, Netanyahu consummates the new capitalist Israel and incarnates an Israel–American partnership as deep and interdependent, and potentially as procreative, as any marriage. Out of it can emerge a new twenty-first century Judeo–Christian alliance in economics, culture, military capabilities, and even religion.

Netanyahu comes from the most Zionist of families. On both sides, his grandparents fled to Palestine long before the establishment of Israel. Then called Mileikowsky, his father's forebears came in 1920, while his mother's Marcus ancestors arrived a generation earlier, in 1896. On both sides, oral history and epistolary tradition describes the almost empty land they settled. Netanyahu describes his mother's grandfather planting almond trees during the day and poring through the Talmud at night. As he wrote, "By the time my mother was born in nearby Petah Tikva ('Gate of Hope') in 1912, the family was living, amid orchards they had planted, in a fine house with a promenade of palm trees leading up to it." The desert bloomed for Netanyahu's maternal forebears.

A more intellectual inspiration for the future prime minister was his paternal grandfather Nathan Mileikowsky, who though no tiller of the arid land became one of the most eloquent and compelling figures in the history of Zionism. Born in Lithuania in 1880, he was ordained a rabbi at age eighteen and emerged as a highly sought-after global lecturer by the age of twenty, a charismatic orator and "a fiery tribune of the [Jewish] people," who already at the time was proclaiming in speeches from Warsaw, Poland, to Harbin, China, the concept of settlement that his grandson upholds today.

Described by a Jewish journalist as a "genius," who "with the breadth of his imagination…has the ability to raise his listeners to the highest ecstasy," Mileikowsky found himself trapped in Poland when it fell under German control early in World War I. The Germans proposed to send him to America to enlist US Jews in a drive to keep America out of the war. Though proffered a "vast" payment by the German governor, he refused to comply unless the Kaiser would endorse a Jewish state in Palestine and press the Ottoman Turks to relinquish the territory over which they ruled. When no such deal could be achieved, Mileikowsky stayed in Poland until 1920, when he took his wife Sarah and their eight young children to Palestine, where he changed the family name to Netanyahu (meaning "given by God"). Eschewing any return to the soil, he accepted a missionary role as a manager of the Jewish National Fund, first in Europe and then in the United States. Here he encountered the eminent Zionist leader, Ze'ev Jabotinsky, who envisaged Israel "on both sides of the Jordan." As a young man, the prime minister's father Benzion became Jabotinsky's assistant in the United States until the famed Zionist's death at sixty in 1940.

Although left-leaning historians and journalists generally describe Jabotinsky and the elder Netanyahus, Nathan and Benzion, as extremists and reactionaries, the subsequent history of Israel vindicates their "Greater Israel" vision over the more accommodating posture of David Ben-Gurion, Golda Meir, and their followers. The prevailing notion of a diminutive Israel, with its constant offers to give up yet more land for peace, and with regular unilateral relinquishments of territory, has won the Israelis no gratitude or support whatsoever in the international community and has achieved little discernible peace.

Netanyahu's Zionist roots and fiery passion for his country implies no parochial patriotism. More than any other foreign leader and even more than many American politicians, he is immersed in American political culture and has deeply influenced the American political debate. After his graduate studies in business at MIT, and government at Harvard, he went to work at the Boston Consulting Group (BCG) at the height of its influence and success in the late 1970s. Under the leadership of Bruce Henderson, carried on in a spin-off company by William Bain, BCG developed the learning curve and explained the resulting competitive dynamics of price cuts. BCG taught that aggressive price cuts and the attendant increase in unit volume of sales are the most effective strategies in business, leading to a cascade of benefits, including greater market share, lower costs, higher margins, and competitive breakthroughs on the learning curve as larger production volumes yield experience. Fully aware of the close analogy with the dynamic global impact of tax-rate reductions, the BCG analysts supplied the most sophisticated version of the microeconomics of supply-side philosophy.

Working at BCG for two years, Netanyahu grasped the underlying assumptions of supply-side tax cuts as early as any American politician, including Jack Kemp and Ronald Reagan. During the early 1980s, in the heyday of the Reagan administration, Netanyahu served as the dashing and flamboyant political *attaché* to the Israeli Embassy in Washington, where he became a media favorite and friend of key members of the Reagan circle such as Kemp and Reagan's secretary of state, George Schultz, as well as his UN ambassador, Jeane Kirkpatrick. A cynosure for leading American Jewish businessmen, notably Ronald Lauder and Sheldon Adelson, he was willing to debate any of Israel's critics, such as Columbia University's Palestinian apologist Edward Said, and was able to crush most and hold his own with all. From his Washington post, he went on to become Israeli's ambassador to the United Nations, extending his charismatic presence to New York. Among his myriad of fans were talk-show host Larry King and John Stossel of ABC News.

All in all, the Netanyahu family has been more successful in the United States than in Israel. Not only did his father Benzion attain his greatest eminence as a historian of the Spanish Inquisition teaching at Cornell, but no fewer than six of Benzion's brothers became steel tycoons in the United States under the name Milo, which they adopted upon immigrating to America.

Bibi always kept in touch with his American uncles, and after hearing him speak on terrorism before a joint session of Congress after 9/11, his Uncle Zachary proudly observed that if his nephew had not been born in Tel Aviv, he might have become the first Jewish president of the United States. After his May 2011 appearance before a joint session of the US Congress, Republicans spoke longingly of finding a birth certificate for him somewhere in the file cabinets of some Pennsylvania town.

As prime minister in the 1990s and finance minister under Ariel Sharon from 2003 to 2005, Netanyahu led the drive to liberate and recast the Israeli economy as the leading force for prosperity in the Arab world—if only the Arabs would see it. Even if his dream of a transformation of the regional economy succeeds, however, no legacy of tax cuts, hedge fund performance fees, and single taxation of venture investors would prompt anyone to talk of Netanyahu in the same breath as Winston Churchill. Netanyahu's Churchillian role and *reveille* has come on the issue of Islamist terrorism and the Iranian nuclear threat: the global jihad against the United States and Israel. Just as Churchill gained a prophetic advantage by paying close attention to the early rhetoric of Adolf Hitler and his disciples, Netanyahu understands that the best way to grasp the intentions of organizations such as al-Qaida, Hezbollah, Hamas, and the Iranian mullahs is to listen to what they have to say.

Even more than Churchill, Netanyahu has been a warrior since his early years. Before entering college, he joined the elite General Staff

Reconnaissance Unit—the secret Sayeret Matkal—or "269," that served as a spearhead for the Israel Defense Forces in their combat against terrorism. It was this unit that later led a retaliatory attack against the perpetrators of the 1972 Munich Olympic Village attack on Israeli athletes by killing three of their leaders. Among the targets of his first operation with the unit, in 1968, in response to a mine attack on a bus full of young Israelis, was Yasser Arafat. The Palestinian leader was targeted for capture by a paratroop recon team, while Netanhayu's unit rescued injured members of an ambushed tank team. Arafat managed to escape disguised as a woman.

Toward the end of 1968, Netanyahu participated in a successful counter-terror operation against Middle East Airlines and Libyan Arab Airlines, destroying fourteen unoccupied planes at the Beirut International Airport in retaliation for an attack by Palestinian terrorists. Members of the Popular Front for the Liberation of Palestine had arrived in Athens from Beirut airport and fired on an El Al jet, killing an Israeli citizen, wounding a stewardess, and damaging the aircraft. Netanyahu also played a key role in securing the release of forty hostages from a hijacked Sabena Airlines plane at the Ben-Gurion Airport. (He was wounded in the arm by accidental friendly fire.)

In May 1969, he nearly lost his life in an action against Egyptian forces that had been laying traps for the Israelis near the Suez Canal. The team succeeded in destroying an Egyptian truck loaded with weapons, but two days later Egyptian troops opened fire on Netanyahu's inflated rubber boat operating in the canal. Laden with ammunition for his machine gun, Netanyahu discovered that he could neither swim nor disengage himself from his sling full of ammunition. He had all but drowned by the time he was rescued by a naval commando named Israel Assaf, who happened to notice bubbles of foam on the surface, felt for a head under the water, and extracted Netanyahu by his hair under intense Egyptian fire.

A major impetus for Netanyahu's unyielding emphasis on the terrorist threat was the death of his brother Jonathan who had led the key commando rescue team at Entebbe in Uganda in 1976. A group of seven terrorists had seized an Air France Airbus on a flight to Paris from Tel Aviv. Bearing guns and grenades, they forced the pilot to fly to Libya to refuel, and then land at Entebbe 2,500 miles from Tel Aviv. Declaring the principle of no compromise with terror, Prime Minister Yitzhak Rabin ordered the elite unit to fly to Entebbe, kill the terrorists, free the 103 Jewish hostages who remained after the gentile passengers had been released, and bring them home. The operation was a stunning success. Only three hostages were killed in the fighting. An additional hostage—an elderly woman who had become ill in Uganda—could not be rescued because she had been taken to a hospital in Kampala; she was later murdered in her hospital bed under the orders of the brutal Ugandan dictator, Idi Amin. But Jonathan Netayahu, guiding his troops from outside the terminal, was shot dead by a Ugandan soldier from the top of the airport control tower.

This experience transformed Netanyahu's life, somewhat in the way that the death of Joseph P. Kennedy Jr. in World War II changed the life of his brother John F. Kennedy. In the United States at the time, Benjamin Netanyahu resolved to enter politics, with a focus on combating terrorism.

After founding the Jonathan Institute, Netanyahu called a conference on terrorism in July 1979 in Jerusalem. He attracted such notables as George H. W. Bush, then a former head of the CIA, as well as future Reagan cabinet leaders George Schultz and Ed Meese, then-FBI Director William Webster, and soon-to-be American ambassador to the UN, Jeane Kirkpatrick. To this group Netanyahu offered shocking details of a Soviet network of training camps for Muslim terrorists.

Out of this conference came Netanyahu's first book, an edited compilation of the speeches from the event together with two analytical chapters by the editor. It was called *International Terrorism: Challenge and Response; Proceedings of the Jerusalem Conference on International Terrorism.* The second conference was held at the Four Seasons Hotel in Washington, DC, in 1984, and attracted another group of luminaries and produced another notable book, *Terrorism: How the West Can Win,*

THE ISRAEL TEST

also edited and with an introduction by Netanyahu. Highly impressed, George Schultz gave the book to Ronald Reagan, and he is said to have read it later on a plane to Asia. Then in 1995, Netanyahu wrote his own book, *Fighting Terrorism: How Democracies Can Defeat the International Terrorist Network,* which was republished after 9/11 with a foreword consisting of his September 20, 2001, speech to Congress.

Netanyahu singlehandedly shaped the US response to terror of three American administrations. Like Churchill, he took his enemies at their own word and resolved to overcome them, whatever it might take. His own first administration ended in three years with an economic crisis caused by the bursting of the tech bubble, and he was defeated in a sweep by his former special forces commander, Ehud Barak. But both Netanyahu's economic policies and his view of terrorism were vindicated by subsequent events.

Netanyahu is a flawed politician, but he is flawed like Churchill—stogies and drink (though Bibi is a teetotaler compared to Churchill's famed capacity) and a succession of three wives. Like Churchill, Netanyahu was more than a decade ahead of his contemporaries in grasping that Israel's enemies are serious and that their stated goals must be weighed seriously. Now he must confront the Iranians at a time when it appears that the only plausible path is the overthrow of their government. Perhaps, though, there is an implausible alternative.

"The first and most crucial thing to understand [about terrorism]," as Netanyahu told the US Congress after 9/11, is that "there is no international terrorism without the support of sovereign states... Terrorists are not suspended in midair. They train, arm, and indoctrinate their killers from within safe havens in the territories provided by terrorist states." The reality is that Hezbollah and Hamas are creatures of Iran, that al-Qaida is harbored by Pakistan, that the Palestinian Authority depends on Egypt, Saudi Arabia, and the United Nations, and that the Kurdish PKK, the Islamic jihad, and Hamas all subsist on Syrian support. North Korea aids Iran and Pakistan in their nuclear ambitions, which portend the most lethal threat that terrorism poses.

162

Even suicide bombings, as Netanyahu observes, "are seldom carried out by solitary individuals. A whole array of people inculcate the suicide, provide him with explosives, guide him in their use, select the chosen target, arrange for his undetected arrival there, and promise to take care of his family after the deed is done. In short, suicide attacks require a significant infrastructure, and the people who provide it are anything but suicidal." These people are all ensconced in nation-states, and within communities and are taught, sustained, encouraged and their families financially rewarded by them. In addition, he explains, the "terrorist states and terror organizations together form a terror network, whose constituent parts support each other operationally as well as politically."

Netanyahu spurns the romantic image of the lone caveman terrorist who poses a mere police problem. As the late Boston University strategist Angelo Codevilla explained, this concept "substitute[s] in our collective mind the soft myth that terrorism is the work of romantic rogues for the hard reality that it can happen only because certain states want it to happen or let it happen."

The influence on US policy of Netanyahu's great insight has been both profound and lamentably limited. When George W. Bush responded to 9/11 by finally dropping the cops-and-robbers model of fighting terrorism, focusing instead on punishing the Taliban, the state sponsors of 9/11, he was following Netanyahu's prescription. Far more so than the pursuit of Osama bin Laden, the exemplary termination of the Taliban regime was the crucial response to 9/11, defining the risk to any state sponsors contemplating attacks on the United States.

Missing Netanyahu's message and perpetuating the myth of stateless terrorism is the US practice of declaring war on something called "terror" while continuing to offer foreign aid and prestige to the very governments that enable and sponsor actual terrorist acts. Apart from drug dealing, none of the terrorist organizations has any substantial means of internal support. None is capable of running a country that partakes of the productive activities of humankind. Most of them run front organizations as shells for the collection of money from the West in a kind of global shakedown racket. As Michael Yon shows in his devastating portrait of al-Qaida in his book, *Moment of Truth in Iraq*, the terrorists' grip on the local population is driven more by fear and dependency than by any heartfelt unity.

Sustaining this terrorist network of states is largely foreign aid to governments, together with environmental bars to energy production in the West that endow despots with economic power. Terrorism will continue as long as these literally suicidal Western policies continue. Without the support of the United Nations and US foreign aid, many of the mendicant oppressor states of the Third World would wither away, liberating their people to join the adventure of productive capitalism.

Netanyahu's message is that terrorist nations are not strong. They are pathetically weak. His counsel is to "oppose the bad things when they are small." Libya during the Qaddafi era was perhaps the leading perpetrator of terrorism, financing assassinations and bombings around the globe and killing Libyan exiles in the West. An effective program of sanctions against Libya coupled with the exclamation point of a bombing led to a rapid, albeit impermanent, change in Libyan policy by persuading Gaddafi to give up his nuclear weapons.

Terrorists gain all their power and momentum from the compulsive "negotiations," the multipronged founts of foreign aid, the "peace-keeping" forces, and the legal contortions of the cowering West. As Netanyahu points out, "Terrorism has the unfortunate quality of expanding to fill the vacuum left to it by passivity or weakness." But this murderous momentum, feeding on the pacifist flailing and self-abuse and outflung alms and oblations of the West, will rapidly reverse when faced with resolute resistance. He writes: "Once the terrorists know that virtually the entire population will stand behind the government's decision never to negotiate with them, the possibility of actually extracting political concessions [from the West] will begin to look exceedingly remote." The terrorist afflatus will dissipate and the momentum can be reversed.

In a bold moment during a joint press conference with President Obama, Netanyahu performed a Churchillian role. He told the president and the American people:

"We've been around for almost 4,000 years. We have experienced struggle and suffering like no other people. We've gone through expulsions and pogroms and massacres and the murder of millions.

"But I can say that even at the dearth of—even at the nadir of the valley of death, we never lost hope and we never lost our dream of re-establishing a sovereign state in our ancient homeland, the land of Israel. And now it falls on my shoulders as the prime minister of Israel at a time of extraordinary instability and uncertainty in the Middle East to work with you to fashion a peace that will ensure Israel's security and will not jeopardize its survival.

"I take this responsibility with pride but with great humility, because, as I told you in our conversation, we don't have a lot of margin for error and because, Mr. President, history will not give the Jewish people another chance."

America's enemies understand deeply and intuitively that no US war aims or resources in the Middle East are remotely as important as Israel, with its ever-growing panoply of technical, economic, moral, and military assets.

Under the leadership of Netanyahu, Israel cruised through the global slump with scarcely a down quarter and no deficit or stimulus package. It has steadily increased its global supremacy, behind only the United States, in an array of leading-edge technologies. During a period of water crises around the globe, it is incontestably the world leader in water recycling and desalinization. During an epoch when all the world's cities, from Seoul to New York, face the threat of terrorist rockets, Israel's battle tested "Iron Dome" provides a unique answer based on original inventions in microchips that radically reduce the weight and cost of the interceptors. Israel has also made major advances in longer-range missile defense, robotic warfare, and unmanned aerial vehicles that can stay aloft for days. In the face of global campaigns to boycott its goods, and an ever-ascendant shekel, it raised its exports 19.9 percent in 2010's fourth quarter and 27.3 percent in the first quarter of 2011 and continued to expand its prowess through the new decade.

Spurring the entire US information sector, Israelis supply Intel corporation with many of its advanced microprocessors, Cisco with core router designs and realtime programmable network processors for the next generation Internet, Apple with robust miniaturized solid state memory systems for its iPhones, iPods, and iPads, and Microsoft with critical user interface designs for the OS7 product line and the Kinect gaming motion sensor interface, the fastest rising consumer electronic product in history. Leading American companies, from General Electric and Johnson & Johnson to IBM and Berkshire Hathaway, continue to rely on Israeli labs and inventions for some of their fastest growing products and most promising projects.

Vital to the American economy and military capabilities, tiny Israel's unparalleled achievements in industry and intellect have conjured up the familiar anti-Semitic frenzies among all the economically and morally failed societies of the socialist and Islamist Third World, from Iran to Venezuela. They all imagine that by delegitimizing, demoralizing, defeating or even destroying Israel, they could take a major step toward bringing down the entire capitalist West.

To most sophisticated Westerners, the jihadist focus on Israel seems bizarre and counterproductive and their dreams of wider conquest simply demented. But on the centrality of Israel, the jihadists have it right. Unmoored from the paramount goal of deterring attacks on Israel or defending it against the common enemy, US Mideast strategy has devolved into incoherence. It drifts from a futile and confusing funambulism among the tribes of Afghanistan to arming the Hizbollah-linked Lebanese Army with sophisticated night fighting gear, Obama's delivering pallets of cash worth $1.7 billion to Iran, followed by Biden's additional $10 billion to Iran in 2023, enhancing the Palestinian police forces with a hundred million dollars worth of new equipment and training assistance, and propping up the new virulently anti-Israel Egyptian regime, all while supposedly guaranteeing military superiority to Israel. This quixotic balancing act is sure to boomerang in the case of a new war that such a Janus-faced policy will make both more likely and more lethal.

Stultifying all US policy is a crippling preoccupation with the claimed grievances of the Palestinians and their supposed right to a state of their own in the West Bank and Gaza. But history moves on and at a certain point becomes irretrievable. When the US and the UN endorsed and financed Yassir Arafat's return from Tunisia in 1993 and delivered the territories into the sanguinary hands of a jihadist cult led by this fervent admirer of Hitler's *Mein Kampf*, the "two-state solution" became a suicide pact for Israel. When the PLO launched two murderous intifadas within a little over a decade, responded to withdrawals from southern Lebanon and from Gaza with scores of thousands of rockets on Israeli towns, spurned every sacrificial offer of "Land for Peace" from Oslo through Camp David, reversed the huge economic gains fostered in the Territories between 1967 and 1990, and allowed the rabid anti-Semitic ascendancy of Hamas in Gaza and Hizbollah in Lebanon, the die was cast.

As current Palestinian leaders continue to name city squares after the most murderous suicide bombers, continue to indoctrinate generations of Palestinian youth in school with a genocidal ideology that reduces Jews to a subhuman status of "rodents and vermin," we can finally say we get the message. Regardless of what Netanyahu may have said in his ritual attempts to placate Obama, Israel cannot allow a Palestinian state to be embedded in its heart like a tumescent malignancy.

If the Palestine Authority wants to make a deal, it should try negotiating with Jordan, already a dominantly Palestinian state four times larger than Israel and with one tenth the population density. Or they can try to shake down Syria or Egypt. The Israelis are moving on. We should follow.

For the US, moving on means a sober recognition that Israel is not too large but too small. A booming economy still absorbing overseas investment and a substantial net inflow of immigrants, squeezed into a space the size of New Jersey, hemmed in by enemies on three sides, with sixty thousand Hizbollah and Hamas rockets at the ready, and Iran lurking with nuclear ambitions and genocidal intent over the horizon, Israel obviously needs every acre it now controls, including buffer zones in Judea, Samaria, and the Golan Heights. Despite its huge technological advances, its survival continues to rely on peremptory policing of the West Bank, on an ever advancing shield of antimissile technology, and on the unswerving commitment of the United States.

But this is no one-way street. At a time of economic doldrums, debt overhang, suicidal energy policies, and venture capitalists who hope to sustain the US economy and defense with Facebook pages and X (formerly Twitter) feeds, US defense and prosperity increasingly depend on the ever growing financial, military, and technological power of Israel. Together we stand and we can deter or defeat every foe.

This choice sums up our Israel Test today. We must meet it. Failure will doom the West to decadence in a long demoralized war against ascendant jihadist barbarians, with demographics and nuclear weapons on their side, and no assurance of US victory.

The fight against terror must be a joint effort between the United States and Israel. Netanyahu epitomizes the unity of the United States and Israel. His role dramatizes Israel as, in effect, an independent military projection for America's front line into enemy-targeted territory, an extension of Silicon Valley, a font of our Judeo–Christian roots, a source of American genius. Over the years, from the time of Harry Truman, who boldly recognized the Israeli state against his pusillanimous State Department with its long-held Arabist sympathies, through the era of Nixon and Kissinger during the Yom Kippur War in 1973, to the eras of Ronald Reagan and George W. Bush, the United States has often come to the defense of Israel. Today, in the continuing war on jihadi terror, the United States needs the leadership and guidance of Netanyahu as much as Israel needs the United States in their combined battle for the very survival of Western civilization.

CHAPTER ELEVEN

LAND FOR WAR

The crucial assumption of the Peace Now movement is that it is within Israel's power to choose peace, that there is something that Israel can give, a price it can pay that would finally and fully purchase peace.

This price is widely believed to be expressed in land. The utterly conventional and obviously fantastic consensus view of nearly all authorities on the subject, reflected in the policies of most of the world's governments led by the United States, is that the key problem in the Mideast is that Israel has too much land. Their remedy is therefore for Israel to give up land, mostly to a Palestinian state as envisioned by these same experts. Awarded to the current Palestinian regime or to some similar successor, the result would be another fanatical anti-Jewish Muslim nation-state with no identity to sustain it beyond the Palestinian sense of eternal grievance and hatred of Israelis.

The dream of land for peace enchants Westerners precisely because it appears to embody all the directness, legality and simplicity of a purely commercial transaction, suggesting that some price—this many square miles or that—would close the deal to everyone's satisfaction and reveal jihad to be nothing more and nothing less than a negotiating position to be terminated at will when the Israelis, at long last, pay up. Whether appeasement or extortion, the rationale hardly matters. After all, according to the stereotypes, Jews for millennia have bridled at extortion and then paid up as the price of doing business.

The evidence of tens of billions of dollars in tribute collected from the Israelis and the West since the perfidious 1993 Oslo Accords constitute ample proof, if any were needed, that the Palestinian Authority is indeed an extortion racket. But the object of the racket has nothing to do with a few square miles of disputed land in the territories. The Palestinian regime has as little interest in land as it has in peace.

The so-called "peace" process negotiations themselves confirm this observation. The sense that, by rational "commercial" standards, the parties are so close to agreement that, as Tzipi Livni would have it, "the dove is on the windowsill," powerfully sustains the land-for-peace illusion. With so little left to give, according to the negotiating maps, Israel could attain peaceful coexistence with only minor concessions. The implication is that the Palestinians and their backers in the Arab world have waged jihad for decades, brought death and poverty and terror on their own land and people, and unceasingly pledged death to Israel and every Jew in its domain, as a negotiating tactic in pursuit of a fractionally better real estate deal.

Such a belief borders on insanity. As the American-born Israeli author, David Meir-Levi, explains, "From 1949 to 1967 there were no settlements in the West Bank or the Gaza Strip. Nor was there peace. The settlements to which the Arabs objected at that time were Tel Aviv, Haifa, Hadera, Afula, etc.—in other words the settlement of Israel itself." That is still the stance of the Arabs and Iranians who count.

Why, then, do many Israelis, including most governments since 1967, seem to take this land-for-peace canard seriously?

The answer is to be found in another tenacious illusion: the always treacherous chimera of racialist self-determination, the most bewitching of all *ersatz* democratic ideologies and democracy's paramount enemy for more than 150 years.

Israel is not racist and has imposed no racial standards in its own democracy. Arabs and Christians sit in the democratically-elected Knesset and serve in its army. Instead, the Israelis are the people in the world most universally and passionately accused of racism by—racists. Clinging together for safety, the Jews are reviled as clannish and chauvinistic conspirators. Jews often battle the libel by internalizing it, overcompensating for the accusation of tribalism by lowering the defenses of the tribe in the face of its enemies—the mostly Arab regimes that are the leading protagonists of the Jew-hating cause in our time.

Goading Israel into this cul-de-sac of racial democracy is the "demographic threat," as neatly summed up in a May 2008 *Atlantic* magazine cover story by Jeffrey Goldberg entitled "Is Israel Finished?" What terrifies Goldberg is the prospect that "within the next several years, the number of Arabs under Israeli control—there are now more than 1.3 million Arab citizens of Israel (there are 5.4 million Jews), and an additional 3.4 million or more Arabs who live in the West Bank and Gaza—will be greater than the number of Jews." He cites a much-contested Israeli estimate that "by 2020, Jews will make up just 47 percent of the people who live between the Jordan River and the Mediterranean Sea." By extending Israel's domains beyond the regions where Jews outnumber Arabs, Goldberg and his ilk believe, the settlements jeopardize both the Jewish majority and Israeli legitimacy.

Goldberg's solution is essentially to uproot the some 400,000 Jewish inhabitants in the West Bank and Eastern Jerusalem. You read that right. The expert's solution is to remove 400,000 people not only from their homes, but from their communities, the schools and synagogues they built, and the roads and infrastructure they created.

Goldberg's article justifies this brutal and ignominious surrender by suggesting that, together with the demographic trend, the West Bank settlements are "a catastrophe." Echoing Jimmy Carter's libelous sentiment in his book, *Palestine: Peace Not Apartheid*, Goldberg even raises fears that "Israel will become a state like pre-Mandela South Africa, in which the minority ruled the majority."

Clinching the argument, in Goldberg's deluded view, he writes: "If the Arabs of the West Bank and Gaza were given the vote, then Israel, a country whose fundamental purpose has been to serve as a refuge for persecuted Jews, and allow those Jews to have the novel experience of being part of a majority, would disappear, to be replaced by an Arab-dominated 'bi-national' state."

Goldberg should be reassured. Judging from the behavior of virtually all other Arab states, any such bi-national state would be short-lived. An Arab-run Israel would quickly expel all its Jews and thus cripple its capitalist economy. Goldberg and Company's notion of the rules of democracy amounts to an Israeli suicide pact.

In ceding territory to its enemies and conceding the claims of the racial parodists of democracy, Israel would betray not only herself, her children, and her Zionist forebears but also democracy and the West itself. It is precisely by resisting the era's most popular racialist perversion of the democratic idea that Israel defines, defends, vindicates, and illuminates democracy's true meaning. To the extent that Israel instead concedes the claims of mere ethnic majoritarianism, Israel betrays the democratic idea.

Elections—counting heads rather than breaking them—are a prime tool of democracy, but hardly its essence. Far from the arbitrary dictate of the latest election, democracy denotes the enduring self-rule of a people assumed to be equal under the Lord and the law. Elections every day would not make a democracy of a society in which the decisive political forces are teenage gangs with guns and terrorist courtiers doling out foreign aid to an intimidated populace.

No tenable theory of democracy allows the majority to destroy or expropriate the minority. Without a functioning and legally protected capitalist system, democracies swiftly sink into ochlocracies, ruled by the mob, not the duly-elected. Without the independent private sources of power imparted by free businesses, unbiased courts, and other institutions of economic order, any democracy becomes a despotism ruled by any tribe of thug politicians that manages to gain control. If it has oil or foreign aid, the regime may stay in power for decades, if not centuries. The failure of Israeli intellectuals and politicians (and their US counterparts) to comprehend this reality is far more lethal than any predicted demographic trend.

Americans, above all, should understand this matter since it echoes the central trial of American history. As Lewis Lehrman wrote in *Lincoln at Peoria*, his book on the 1854 speech that launched Lincoln's career as the nemesis of slavery, the decisive issue between the future president and his rival Stephen Douglas was the limits of popular sovereignty. Do majority rights extend to the right to enslave minorities?

This is the very issue that currently convulses the Middle East and animates the Israel Test. By claiming the right to banish or kill 7.2 million Jews, Arab leaders assert the supremacy of majorities to the point of enabling them to dispossess and displace and, indeed, to annihilate minorities. By supporting the expulsion of Jews from the West Bank and Gaza, American critics of Israel such as Jeffrey Goldberg and Thomas L. Friedman in principle accept this "democratic" imperative. Such a "democracy" of "one man, one vote, one time" can establish communism, Nazism, or any other kind of human enslavement.

Even including the West Bank and Gaza, Israel is a tiny country. This "empire," this domineering colonialist, constitutes one-sixth of one percent of the Middle Eastern land mass. The Jewish one-tenth of the West Bank population lives on about 2 percent of that area with perhaps another 4 percent reserved for roads and security. Minus the settled territories, Israel is nine miles wide at its narrowest point between the West Bank and the Mediterranean Sea. That's fourteen and a half kilometers, a distance that can be crossed by a runner, or a modern tank, in under an hour.

An expulsion of Israelis from the West Bank would merely repeat the suicidal harvest of the previous Israeli flight from southern Lebanon and Gaza. Both capitulations led to the triumph of bristling deadly tyrannies, Hezbollah and Hamas, financed by Iran and institutional foreign aid. The surrender of the West Bank would be even more deadly, since its mountainous spine would provide Israel's enemies with an elevated staging area for a sudden invasion that could destroy the country.

Making a fetish of Israel's pre-1967 borders, both President Obama and former President Jimmy Carter pompously proclaimed them unimpeachably "legal," embodied in the notorious UN resolution 242 in 1967 and UN resolution 338 in 1973, and accepted at Camp David in 1978 and in Oslo in 1993 by both Arabs and Israelis. Carter's entire work is one perplexed and disgruntled screed against the Israelis for failing to observe their legal confinement. But Israel's agreement to accept most of the pre-1967 borders has always been contingent and must always be contingent on verifiable guarantees of its defense. Legal or not, those borders—so constricted that they have been termed "Auschwitz borders"—left Israel as an indefensible shard.

The pre-1967 borders have been fully tested. Whether an attractive nuisance or an irresistible temptation, their vulnerability resulted in concerted attacks from three neighboring Arab states in 1967. Regardless of agreements or legalities, all the documents affirming the pre-1967 borders have been perforated and rescinded by the Arabs and their bullets, mortars, grenades, and bombs in four wars and innumerable raids and missile attacks.

A country surrounded by friendly neighbors could tolerate a nine-mile-wide waist guaranteed by the sort of "solemn pledges" that impress people like Jimmy Carter and Barack Obama. But less than worthless are solemn pledges from Arab regimes that have trained their people for most of a century, from madrasahs to military drills to maniacal media screeds, that Israel is a diabolical expression of a verminous bacterial subhuman population.

Under these conditions, with a relentlessly indoctrinated electorate, jihadist democracy is the enemy. This intrinsically anti-democratic die was cast long ago by rabid anti-Semitic venom injected daily in Arabic for decades. Israel must command a defensible territory. That means expanded settlements and police constabulary on the mountainous spine of the West Bank and the Golan Heights that afford strategic access to Israel. It means police presence in the Gaza Strip, a frequent source of attacks on Israel.

Thomas L. Friedman, Shlomo Ben-Ami, and others believe the strategic situation changed radically with the emergence of missile technology, such as the Scuds that were successfully aimed at Israel to wild Palestinian applause during the first Iraq war in 1991. With Israel, like the United States and all other modern nations, reachable from afar, these writers contend that the country no longer needs to hold a buffer of settlements to protect itself from nearby enemies. With Palestinians living among Israelis, the threat is no longer from outside but from within.

Benjamin Netanyahu rebuts this view in his book, *A Durable Peace*: "The lesson for a small country like Israel is this: In the age of missiles territory counts more, not less. Long-range missiles increase the need for mobilization time, and short-range missiles can destroy strategic targets within their reach. For both reasons, the control of a contiguous buffer area becomes more, not less, important." He quotes the left-oriented Jaffee Center for Strategic Studies in Tel Aviv: "Territory is especially vital when it permits our forces to 'buy' time: in case of a surprise attack, this enables us to mobilize our reserves and bring them to the front lines before the aggressor succeeds in taking any part of our vital area."

Even if Netanyahu's argument were undermined by some new technology or strategy, the moral and democratic case is clear. Both the history of invasion and the present commitment of the Arabs to the annihilation of Israel vindicate Israel's absolute and unilateral right to decide what land it must keep and what it may cede to the Palestinians, and under what conditions. Israel has no prior obligation to cede a single square inch of land except to advance its own security. If the right answer for Israel is to rule for a thousand years the territories on which reside enemies committed to its destruction, then no true principle of democracy compels them to do otherwise.

This confusion about the true nature and requirements of democracy enervates most of Israel's would-be advocates even as it emboldens its enemies. Perhaps the most influential writer on these issues is Thomas L. Friedman, who has combined all his illusions into a grand mythology. From his *New York Times* columns to his earlier book *From Beirut to Jerusalem*, which provided perhaps the most compulsively readable and courageously researched guidebook to this conflict, he insists that the obstacle to peace is not Arab violence but Israeli bellicosity.

In his book, he tells the story of his arrival in Beirut in 1982 as a committed Zionist since childhood and the tale of his eventual disillusionment. Before his eyes, Beirut became a snake pit of contending factions. When Yasser Arafat led the Palestinians into southern Lebanon as a vantage to attack Israel, it upset the balance between Maronite Christians and Muslims who had shared power. Muslims became a decisive majority. Because the Muslims as a majority had no tradition or intention of granting rights to minorities, the new situation was intolerable to the Maronites. Attacks came from all sides. While he was away, Friedman's apartment building was blown up with his driver's wife and children inside. Suicide bombs from the Iranian-financed terrorists of Hezbollah destroyed both the US embassy and US Marines' headquarters.

The climax came in 1983 after the assassination by the PLO of the mildly pro-Israel Lebanese prime minister, Bashir Gemayel. Friedman reported a retaliatory massacre of some 400 or more Palestinians at the refugee camps at Sabra and Shatila, near Beirut, committed by Maronite Christian Phalangists. Israeli soldiers still surrounding the area failed to stop the killings. Challenging the Israelis' claims that they had no foreknowledge of these crimes, his articles seethed with implications of unforgivable complicity. Friedman's series of investigations in the *New York Times* won him a Pulitzer Prize and durably sullied the reputation of the Israel Defense Forces. In a fabulous feat of moral equivalence, many writers compared Israel's behavior in Lebanon with the behavior of the Nazis in Europe.

Probing this scar tissue anew was the Academy Award-nominated Israeli animated documentary, the 2008 *Waltz with Bashir*, directed by Ari Folman, which occasioned many such suggestions by Israeli intellectuals that the most revealing and portentous event of the 1982 Lebanon War was this massacre, supposedly condoned by Israel.

Friedman, the *New York Times,* and the perennially leftist Pulitzer committee were following the venerable tradition in wartime journalism, tested in Vietnam, which holds that the vicissitudes and excesses inevitable in conflict become a saga of one-way scandals and salacious legal investigations. War is terrible, and soldiers of all nations often misstep in the fog. But Israel's offenses in Lebanon, producing perhaps a few thousand civilian casualties, occurred in the middle of a civil war that produced perhaps a half-million deaths. It is invidious and ultimately suicidal for journalists from free nations to focus on a few sensational disputed incidents in the midst of a fifteen-year bloodbath.

Israel occupied southern Lebanon only when it became a terrorist training center for jihadists around the Mideast and a source of repeated attacks on Israel. Regardless of Pulitzer craft and laurels, no reasonable journalistic standard permits the reporter to contemplate a self-defense against extermination and equate it with attacks by genocidal forces.

By stigmatizing the Israeli army and its defense minister Ariel Sharon, Friedman helped make any success in Lebanon impossible. A classic "useful idiot" in Leninist terms, Friedman helped trigger a movement that for a time deprived Israel of one of its greatest leaders and provided new momentum to the Palestinian cause.

Land for peace, however, does have a positive meaning. Beyond the delusional "peace process," there is a vision of the land itself yielding peace as it endows those who live upon it with the raw materials of an orderly and productive life. It is only this goal that makes the proposed exchange of land for peace a credible idea. It is only the notion that the Palestinians might want land on which to make such a peace that suggests Israel might buy peace by giving it to them.

But if the Palestinians seek land for this purpose, why must it come from tiny Israel? The Palestinian Arabs are surrounded on all sides by spacious and compatible Arab countries of which they theoretically could become citizens. Why not the East Bank? That's Jordan, where 300,000 Palestinian Arabs fled during the 1967 war.

A Muslim–Arab state from time to time sustained by Israel and created as a home for the Palestinians, Jordan held the West Bank until King Hussein's treacherous 1967 invasion and shelling of Jerusalem. Jordan retains a far more compelling obligation to these people than does Israel.

Should the Palestinians shun Jordan, perhaps they would prefer the Soviet jihadist state of Syria, which in its guise as "Greater Syria" stretches its reptilian claws throughout the region, including into nearby Lebanon. Egypt is contiguous with Gaza and could easily absorb the Gazan Palestinians who have put their democratic fate into the hands of the terrorists of Hamas and Fatah.

Negotiators with illusions about their adversaries end up negotiating with themselves. Experts on business negotiation advise that "whenever you start negotiating with yourself, you might as well give away the company." This is what the Israelis have been doing for decades, among all their gaggle of solipsistic political parties, each with its fluff of afflatus and acid of animus and symbolic banner of nationhood, each often willing to give away what some other Knesset party cherishes. For the Arabs, these are what-is-ours-is-ours negotiations; what is Israel's is negotiable and is always on the negotiating table

Whatever the Arabs of the jihad and the intifada mean by the word "land" cannot be satisfied by giving up any particular patch of ground. Land to them is less transactional than transcendental, symbolic, and apocalyptic. As with all the ideologies of race and fatherland, all the cults of blood and soil, with all their ruinous and romantic rejections of modernity, inevitably making the Jews their first chosen enemies, they are haunted and driven by demons that no "peace process" can exorcise, much less negotiate out of existence.

Which is not to say that the Arabs are beyond hope or help. Outside observers can easily assume a people are in the grip of a demonic ideology when they are actually only in the grasp of a despotic regime. Obscured in the terror applied by the regime against its own people is the reality that prior to the terrorists' seizure of power, there were other parties in the contest and real majorities for peace and productivity.

In conferring democracy on Germany, or even Japan, to give two much-cited examples, the United States did not miraculously graft alien values onto unwilling nations. The crucial process was not one of conversion at all. It was the total military defeat and destruction of the despotic faction and the transfer of power over time to already strong but long obscured constituencies for capitalist democracy.

Peace can come to the Palestinians tomorrow and nationhood the day after if only they will take what is already in their grasp and go to work. They are prevented from doing this primarily by the rule of a terror regime—it hardly matters whether it calls itself Fatah or Hamas or by a dozen other names—that thrives on violence, chaos and hatred and is kept alive by money from jihadist states, as well as intimidated Western powers and international organizations.

The path to peace is not through negotiations but through invincible rejection of terror, joined to real opportunity for Palestinians who choose life over death. Over the next decades, Israel will grow into the dominant economy in the Middle East and one of the most productive economies in the world. Palestinians must be made to see that displacing Israel is futile, but buying and selling its products and supplying labor for its factories and offices can make Palestinians once again the most successful of all Arabs, as they were between 1967 and 1987. Saved from the Nazi obsessions of their ruling clique, the Palestinians can become major beneficiaries of the emerging new global economy.

CHAPTER TWELVE

TIME FOR THE TEST

As David Gelernter wrote in the *Weekly Standard*, January 19, 2009, "Now, every human being on earth who cares about facts and can tell a lie from a truth knows that there was no such thing as 'Palestinian nationalism' until modern Zionism created it out of whole cloth, by placing enormous value on a piece of land that used to seem as precious to its landlords as a rat-ridden empty lot in a burnt-out neighborhood in the middle of nowhere, in the suburbs of nothing.

"The Jews gradually got possession of an arid stony wasteland...complete with the odd picturesque, crumbling, dirty town; and they loved it. They turned it into a gleaming, thriving, modern nation, not only a military but an intellectual powerhouse.

"And so it is only natural that the former owners' descendants want it back, and remember how much their ancestors loved it, and how the new owners only got possession by wickedness and deceit. Such memories have the strange property of growing clearer instead of cloudier every day....

"There is no irreconcilable difference in the fight between Israel and the Palestinians, no bone-deep dispute that will haunt humanity forever. There is only greed and envy. They never disappear, but can easily move from one target to the next. The problem will be solved as soon as the world stops trying to solve it."

All right. Now it is time for the test.

In the early 1940s in Europe, as Hitler ranted about the depravity of the Jews, the Nazis were already proceeding with the "final solution" that he had promised in *Mein Kampf*. They were preparing concentration camps near railroad lines at Treblinka, Bergen-Belsen, Dachau, Auschwitz, and dozens of other cities. They were lining up railroad cars and gas trucks. They were mobilizing scientists and engineers to develop efficient techniques for the extermination of their fellow human beings. They were transforming a generation of young men into Brown Shirt brigades frothing with hatred and lusting for violence against Jews. They were enlisting foreign allies such as the Grand Mufti Haj Amin al-Husseini to extend the killing to Palestine.

The world, then engulfed by a world war, mostly failed to focus on this particular threat, which seemed too bizarre and evil even to be believed. The West lost six million of its most creative and productive citizens: family members of the same people who shaped twentieth-century science, enabled twentieth-century technology, and opened the horizons for the twenty-first-century economy—the people who largely enabled the West to prevail against the Axis powers and to win the Cold War against the Soviet Union. We have to acknowledge today that in his most ardent cause and most fervent war aim, Hitler largely triumphed. Some sixty-five years later, the number of Jews is still an estimated five million below the number in 1939. Poland, once home to almost 3.5 million Jews, has an estimated Jewish population of only 4,500 as of 2023. As expressed in the compulsive acts of condemnation of Israel in the United Nations, the Nazi obsession has attained a new respectability around the world.

Today, Hitler's rants have morphed into a global program of religious education and military ideology sustained by Arab and Iranian oil money and generous subventions by American taxpayers and the United Nations. The hundreds of thousands of Brown Shirts in Germany have become millions of frothing jihadi youths similarly inculcated with anti-Semitic hatred and a lust for violence. Leading politicians in Iran, Egypt, Syria,

Malaysia, Venezuela, and other nations, and jihadi imams and mullahs around the globe have declared their resolve to destroy Israel.

Unlike the Germans, who faced a formidable technical challenge in carrying out their plan, the incumbent anti-Semites benefit from the increasing availability of nuclear weapons, which could render a new Holocaust both simpler and more efficient than the first. Anti-Semites have the moral support of much of the UN bureaucracy, including its "human rights" apparatus, which is chiefly devoted to anti-Semitic agitprop. The UN General Assembly in 2008 directed 68 percent of its condemnatory resolutions and other strictures against Israel. The UN secretary-general has called for a global boycott of Israel for its efforts to defend itself against new campaigns of extermination. Aiding a new Holocaust is the vulnerability of the state where 7.2 million Jews live, encircled by lethal enemies bent on their annihilation.

Today, the most dangerous form of Holocaust-denial is not rejection of the voluminous evidence of long-ago Nazi crimes but incredulity toward the voluminous evidence of the new Holocaust being planned by Israel's current enemies. Two Iranian presidents have resolved to acquire nuclear weapons for the specific purpose of "wiping Israel off the map." Scores of nations, representing 1.8 billion Muslims, have endorsed the jihad. After the genocidal crimes of World War II and the Communist empire and recent genocidal violence in Rwanda, the Sudan, Somalia, and Zaire, deniers of a new Holocaust agenda manifest a tragic and foolhardy blindness to human nature and human history. Showing no understanding of the central and indispensable contribution of capitalism to human welfare, the world political order is heavily focused on punishing capitalists, as epitomized by Israel and the United States, both maligned as "oppressors."

The problem is not nuclear weapons themselves. They represent another major and irreversible step in the history of weapons development. To condemn them is like condemning meteors, earthquakes, or even the sun. They are now an inexorable part of the world. Moreover, nuclear weapons have a positive aspect. They reflect a generally favorable move of the world from quantitative arms races to qualitative ones, from rivalries of mass mobilization of existing manpower and resources to intellectual competition in the development of new weapons and defenses.

Quantitative arms races focus on diverting wealth from private consumption to public mobilization. Quantitative arms races favor dictatorial regimes with large populations of young men. They reward the ability to extract resources from consumption and re-direct them to the job of reproducing the best existing military tools. Quantitative arms races make a billion youths inculcated with Wahhabi frenzies into a vast and possibly decisive weapon. Quantitative arms races lead either to economic exhaustion or to war.

Qualitative arms races can trump quantitative capabilities. During World War II, the perfection of radar, the emergence of computer decryption, and the mastery of nuclear weapons counteracted the apparently decisive advantages of the Axis nations in existing industrial power and military mobilization. During the Cold War, the advance of US guidance and communications technologies and steps toward effective missile defense countered the massive advantages in manpower of the Soviet Union and the People's Republic of China. In any qualitative rivalry, millions of Jewish individuals and other researchers and inventors operating in free societies can counteract billions of jihadists in mass movements and totalitarian confinement. As the late Canadian-American author and attorney Peter Huber said in an eloquent speech after 9/11, "Our silicon can beat their sons."

Today the superiority of America and its Israeli allies is growing ever greater. The campaigns of the qualitative arms race become increasingly more effective compared to the indoctrination of new Nazis. Hundreds of Talpions can trump millions of Brown Shirts or jihadi youth.

However, there remains an acute danger. Countering the ever-growing American and Israeli lead in new technologies are widespread abolitionist attitudes toward nuclear weapons. Together with hostility toward anti-ballistic missiles, opposition to weapons in space, resistance to civil defense, and blindness to the urgent need for technological answers to nuclear terror, a suicidal pacifism in the United States endangers not only Israel's survival but America's as well.

Echoing the equally corrosive influence of levelers in economics, these attitudes in the West could so inhibit the development of new counter-weapons that a mere quantitative buildup of old weapons systems cobbled together from Western schematics could prevail. A window of opportunity may be opening for rogue powers that can acquire even primitive nuclear weapons. The archaic tools of quantitative competition could trump the superior capabilities of Israel and the West.

Under these conditions, no other single international issue is as important as the nuclear threat to Israel. The case of Israel gives the lie to every notion of unilateral disarmament, every illusion that the adversaries of the West are open to negotiation, every scintilla of belief that our enemies desire peace rather than destruction. Israel is not only a major source of Western technological supremacy and economic leadership—it is also the most vulnerable source of Western power and intelligence. It is not only the canary in the mine shaft—it is also a crucial part of the mine itself.

Over the course of decades, Israel and the United States have made every possible overture toward Israel's enemies, lavishing them with funds, relinquishing land, endorsing Palestinian statehood. If the Arabs or Iranians desired peace, they would long ago have achieved it. There would be a Palestinian state thriving next to Israel. But instead, Israel faces a global mobilization against its very existence. In a world of nuclear weapons, the continued determination to destroy Israel represents a direct threat to New York, Chicago, Houston, Los Angeles and Washington, DC, as well.

In the conflict with the jihadists, inapplicable today are the lessons of the Cold War, during which we carefully learned to live with a nuclear USSR until communism and its empty economy cracked under the pressure of US military advances. During the Cold War, the United States and the Soviet Union learned to live with nuclear weapons by developing a carefully negotiated set of protocols, both in their rhetoric and in their military movements. In relation to Israel, Iran and other jihadist movements are brutally breaching any conceivable definition of protocols. When high officials in major countries announce their intention to use nuclear weapons to "destroy" a nation, they must be addressed in a way that is unnecessary when they threatened "merely" to drive that nation into the sea. All the qualitative resources of the West—all its current military powers and sources of new technology creation—must be brought to bear on the threat.

The defense of Israel must not be reactive. Indeed, it probably cannot even be public. It must mobilize all our resources of intelligence, technology, and surprise. And most important of all, it must succeed.

Like the Germans and Japanese in World War II, our adversaries will not wait for the West to prepare. They will attempt, as they did on 9/11, to achieve surprise. With no qualitative capabilities to cultivate, they know that time is their enemy. Whether against the United States or Israel, they must launch their blows as soon as they are ready.

By eliciting the early declarations and announcements of Iran and other jihadist states, Israel has performed an enormous service to the West. When they can, these countries will obviously assault the Great Satan as well as the Minor Satan. The Israel Test makes the challenge clear. It signals the real predicament of the West.

The predicament of the West is the plight of the world and all its people. The defense of Israel is vital to the defense of the world economy. People are all we have. They are the ultimate resource and the most precious one. Only in peace can they thrive and reproduce.

An inescapable fact of life is that people—and peoples—vary tremendously in their talents and capabilities, and moral integrity, their understanding of the threats against them, their moral courage to face those threats and thus in their capacity to sustain life on earth against nihilist movements such as the jihad. People differ enormously in their ability to conceive the algorithms of economic advance and military defense. Shaped by baffling mixtures of genes and culture, history and faith, civics and law, nations and individuals show a broad spectrum, from an animus for land and blood to an inspiration for creativity and peace.

Just as free economies are necessary for the survival of the human population of the planet, the survival of the Jews is vital to the triumph of free economies. If Israel is subjugated or destroyed, we will have succumbed to forces targeting capitalism and freedom everywhere. We will have willfully permitted a fatal triumph of the barbarian masses whose goals include demoralizing and destroying the United States as well. There are certainly abundant examples that this is already taking place. Any global regime of UN redistribution of resources and suppression of the creators of wealth will doom the globe to a slow retreat to a radically smaller population of far more primitive peoples.

If we have a free, competitive, and collaborative world economy, however, some people and countries will far outperform others. Their outperformance is what makes it remotely possible to feed the current eight billion inhabitants of the planet. As the British science writer, journalist, and businessman Matt Ridley observes in his 2010 book, *The Rational Optimist*, without technological innovations, "we'd have needed about 85 earths to feed 6 billion people... if we'd gone on as 1950 organic farmers without a lot of fertilizer, we'd have needed 82 percent of the world's land area for cultivation, as opposed to the 38 percent that we farm at the moment." Many of the enabling technologies, from desalinization to distributed solar power to targeted irrigation, originated in Israel or were critically advanced there. The United States contributed the world's most potent agricultural machinery and fertilization tools. The universe is hierarchical, and economic freedom is what makes it possible for some humans to climb the hierarchies of knowledge and build systems to sustain life for all other human beings.

Economists and politicians talk of natural endowments, energy supplies, landmasses and sea-lanes, choke points and channels, money supplies and trade balances and capital investment. Environmentalists prattle on about global warming and other alleged planetary disorders. Law professors talk of constitutional penumbra and class action lawsuits and the "freedom to choose."

None of these concerns can hold a candle in importance to the talents of a country's human beings and their commitment to the discipline and devotion to innovation that drive the global economy. What permits the human race to thrive and prosper is the willingness to unleash and affirm the genius of a statistically small number of people: to embrace the encouragement of learning and discovery and collaborate with it rather than succumb to envy and suppress its achievements. The twentieth century was shaped, animated, and endowed largely by a tiny cohort of the earth's population—the Jews. In much of the world, for the majority of the history of the world, they were suppressed and constricted by various dictatorial regimes, some of which they supported. But the achievements of the twentieth century are heavily attributable to the rising prevalence of capitalism in the West and its ability to accommodate the genius of the Jews. Without them, the world would be radically poorer and its prospects for the future would be decisively dimmed.

All around the globe today, however, the leaders of nations and international organizations, prestigious universities, and passionate writers denounce the very countries in which Jews are allowed to create and succeed. These leaders claim to be anti-Zionist, anti-Israel, anti-American, or anti-capitalist, but the distinctions dissolve in the crucial fact of their naked anti-Semitism.

People who obsessively denounce Jews have a historical desgnation: they are Nazis. The Palestinian Arab leaders have shown themselves to be mostly Nazis. Anyone who believes these men should command a nation-state ensconced next to Israel is delusional. There is only one answer to the claims and demands and threats of such people and that answer is "no."

The leaders of Iran are proud Nazis. Anyone who believes that the West can stand aside and conduct amiable negotiations while they acquire access to nuclear weapons is a gull who has failed to learn anything from the history of the twentieth century. The president of Syria is equally obsessed with Jews and Israel. The Wahhabis of Saudi Arabia in their madrasahs around the globe are cultivating new armies of young Brown Shirts. The civilized world must show enough courage of its quondam convictions to answer all the neo-Nazis with a resounding "no."

In the United States, however, most elite opinion believes that this is exactly the moment in human history when disarmament is a desirable option, a moment for intensified concessionary diplomacy in the Middle East, a moment when the supreme issue worthy of domestic and international attention should be "climate change." Such beliefs place the very survival of the United States into question.

The Holocaust threat only begins with Israel. The entire West is vulnerable to the jihad. It can be stopped only through a combination of recognition, resolve, and technology. On the front lines, Israel must face the menace earlier than the United States. Israel has already demonstrated the effectiveness of civil defense programs against missile attacks. By fleeing to underground shelters, by distributing gas masks to every man, woman, and child, Israelis have incurred only a relative handful of deaths—undeniably tragic as each one is—from thousands of strikes on Israeli towns. The Israelis have maintained military forces that long succeeded in holding the jihad at bay.

The Israel Test forces the capitalist world to recognize the necessity of armament and civil defense. Today, the nuclear threat seems chiefly addressed to Israel. But increasing steadily is the potential for importing nuclear weapons into American cities, exploding them offshore near American ports, or detonating bombs above America's critical electronic infrastructure. A nuclear explosion over the central part of the United States might precipitate a cascading electromagnetic pulse that could paralyze the power grid and destroy much of the microchip technology that undergirds our economy. The United States must mobilize all its capabilities of intelligence and defense against these threats.

The Israel Test impels us to forgo the illusion of opting out of the arms race. All too many Americans still subscribe to the "strangest dream" school of international relations, as I called it after singing along to an Ed McCurdy song with Joan Baez at Club 47 on Mount Auburn Street in Cambridge as a college student in the 1960s: *"Last night I had the strangest dream / I ever dreamed before / I dreamed the world had all agreed / To put an end to war / I dreamed I saw a mighty room / The room was filled with men / And the paper they were signing said / They'd never fight again."*

The song and the sentiment are as infectious and deadly as the Oxford peace movement that anesthetized Britain before World War II, as the Peace Now mantra that inebriates Israel and many American Jews who believe themselves to be "supporters" of Israel, as the campaigns for nuclear disarmament that seduce American liberals. The single greatest domestic threat to the United States is not the jihad but the peace movement. Countries that fail to meet the challenge of qualitative armament, of military technology, end up at war.

Ronald Reagan's best moment was his commitment to build antiballistic missiles. His worst, most self-indulgent, and foolish moment was his speech advocating the destruction of nuclear weapons. Regardless of any caveats he included, the speech was a horrible blunder that played into the hands of America's enemies and is still a major weapon in their portfolios. It was his "strangest dream" moment, and if it were to come true, it would doom the country that he loved.

Entirely unsurprisingly, Obama and his pusillanimous successor, Joseph Biden, also entertain this fatuous dream. At moments of particular weakness, Obama spoke of nuclear disarmament. Within a week of assuming office he advocated destroying 80 percent of America's nuclear stockpiles. He contemplated abandoning missile defense. His chief asset in making such proposals was his ability to cite Reagan as a precursor on the road to disarmament. With nuclear weapons in the hands of others and without anti-missiles and lacking, too, other advanced technologies, the United States cannot survive as a free country. Arms races are the inexorable burden of all free peoples.

No major nation in history has succeeded in preserving its integrity and sovereignty without meeting the challenge of ever-advancing armaments. For Israel, the test is obvious. Without maintaining leadership in military technology, the country has no chance at all of survival. But many American intellectuals still imagine that the United States is different, that it is possible or desirable for us to negotiate an "end to the arms race."

Our enemies will always want to end the arms race because they know only free nations can win it. The crucial test of American leadership is to see through the constant stream of proposals for technological disarmament. All our enemies want to confront us without our qualitative superiority.

An end to the arms race would deprive the capitalist countries of their greatest asset in combating barbarism. The result would bring no relief from military competition but rather its transformation. Arms rivalry would shift from qualitative goals that favor free countries such as the United States and Israel toward quantitative rivalry that will favor our barbarian enemies.

AFTERWORD

MY OWN ISRAEL TEST

In the current arenas of controversy, where Israel is a foreign policy issue, a legalistic argument and a historic debate, I am presenting it chiefly as a test. It begins for everyone as a personal test. It is a test that culminates the long experience of American gentiles with Jewish immigration and rivalry. It is a test for American and other Diaspora Jews who wish to proceed with their lives without concern for Middle Eastern conflicts and moral claims. For Jews and gentiles, alike, it is a test now clouded by confusions, evasions, and misunderstandings on all sides. But I believe that the test is clear and definitive.

In the modern capitalist world, in which the historical extremes of poverty have been widely overcome, the most acute moral issues relate to recognition of accomplishment and superiority—treatment not of the poor but of the particularly gifted people whose work is indispensable to providing opportunities for the poor and for everyone else. In capitalism, as I wrote in *Wealth & Poverty* more than forty years ago, the great conflict is not between rich and poor but between incumbent elites and existing forms of capital and the new elites and superior forms of capital that must necessarily displace them if economic progress is to occur.

Thus, the paramount conflict in capitalism is between the established system—entrepreneurs, businesses, political movements, and bureaucracies—and the superior minds and methods, vessels of genius and innovation, that threaten to usurp them. On one side stand the alliances of governments and elites, in democracies and tyrannies alike, which distort economies around the globe by protecting the past in the name of social fashions and special interests. On the other side are the inventors, entrepreneurs, industrial innovators, and visionary artists who challenge every establishment.

The Israel Test revolves around a fact that is recognized by most people in some form, surreptitiously or partially, but is rarely acknowledged openly or explored for its consequences: in any rivalry with intellectual dimensions, disproportionate numbers of both the challengers and of the winners will be Jewish.

Today in America and around the world many of the rich and powerful are Jewish as well. But few people seem to worry much about old money. We have been relatively comfortable with traditional wealth. What is threatening is creative destruction from brilliant and ambitious outsiders. The French have been so preoccupied with this phenomenon that they have supplied us with no fewer than three pejoratives to capture it: the *nouveaux riches, arrivistes,* and the *parvenus.* All three terms apply readily to Jewish immigrants and business successes as well as to Israel, which stands accused of being the newcomer and upstart nation-state in the Middle East.

In most advanced countries, according to the available data, an enormously disproportionate number of brilliant and ambitious outsiders engaged in intellectual and entrepreneurial activities are Jews. Around the globe, wherever freedom opens up, however briefly in historical terms, Jews quickly tend to rise up and prevail. Jews, historically, have shown vigilance in identifying the main chance and courage in taking it. Together with superior knowledge and talent, this visionary audacity is the essence of entrepreneurial prowess. Understanding and combating the rise of anti-Semitism and anti-Zionism requires fathoming the anxious sense of vulnerability of traditional establishments—intellectual, commercial, military, political, and cultural—as they face the Israel Test.

As a youth I learned firsthand the temptations of anti-Semitism. Attending Phillips Exeter Academy in New Hampshire, I devoted nearly all my efforts as a junior to writing for *The Exonian*, the school's daily newspaper, while managing barely to scrape by in my classes. I expected to be named an editor of the school paper for my senior year. For generations, my forebears had been editors. I was entitled. Since virtually no other undergraduate had written as many news stories, feature stories, books reviews, or editorials, I thought my ascension was assured.

When the next editorial board was announced, I was shocked to discover that the editor-in-chief was to be a student named Peter Sobol, whom I had scarcely met and who had contributed nothing notable to the paper. I found that most of the other prospective new editors were also only occasional contributors. Three of them were "New York Jews," as I invidiously observed, who unlike me had achieved high grades, almost effortlessly as it seemed, while I struggled to eke out Cs. If truth be told, at the time they were also more accomplished writers than I.

That summer, in a parental campaign to help me catch up on my studies, I was assigned a Radcliffe student five years my elder as a tutor in the classical languages. In an effort to avoid the famously demanding Exeter courses such as American history and calculus, I was aiming for a Classics diploma. The Radcliffe girl (in those times of atavistic "sexism," we still called female college students "girls") was named Valerie Ann Leval. The name still can suffuse my brain with remembered effervescence and longing.

Enlisted to teach me the Greek language so I could qualify for second-year Greek in my senior year at Exeter, she was a tall, willowy creature, both intelligent and beautiful. On long walks through the fields and over the hills of Tyringham Valley, Massachusetts, I accompanied her in besotted bliss as we recited Greek phrases and conjugated polymorphous Greek verbs from a textbook coauthored by my Exeter teacher.

One day toward the end of the summer, as we strode up a sylvan dirt road by the Gilder Farm in the late afternoon, en route to a hilltop field spread out with mosses and tufted with blueberry bushes and reaching out toward rolling horizons and wide sunset vistas, she asked me how I liked Exeter.

How I ached to impress her! I knew that she would not be taken with callow effusions about the virtues of this famous preparatory school, its oval tables, its fabled teachers, its austere standards. I hesitated to tout Exeter's athletic exploits, my true enthusiasm, to this refined intellectual girl. What to say? We beat Andover 36-0? I chose what seemed to me at the time a path of seductive candor and salty sophistication. Echoing sentiments I had heard both at home and at school, I responded, "Exeter's fine, except that there are too many New York Jews."

At first, Valerie did not reply. We continued crunching up the dirt road. I sensed there was something wrong. My hopes for the evening seemed to be slipping fast away while Valerie contemplated how to respond. Then she commented dryly: "You know, of course, that I am a New York Jew myself."

My stomach turned over like a cement mixer. I gasped and blathered. I cannot remember exactly what it was I said. I suppose I prattled something about all my Jewish friends and my well-known offbeat sense of humor.

To this day I recall the moment as a supreme mortification and as a turning point. Rather than recognizing my shortcomings and inferiority and resolving to overcome them in the future, I had blamed the people who had outperformed me. I had let envy rush in and usurp understanding and admiration. I had succumbed to the lamest of all the world's excuses for failure—blaming the victor. I would pay by losing the respect of this woman I then cared about more than any other. I had flunked my own Israel Test. But I had learned my lesson.

I was brought up in a highly literary and artistic Anglo-Saxon Protestant family in New York City and western Massachusetts. I had learned the family legends. We were classic WASPs all, scions of stained-glass artist Louis Comfort Tiffany, the *Century Magazine* editor Richard

Watson Gilder, Episcopal pastor Reese Fell Alsop of the Church of St. Ann's in Brooklyn Heights, and Chester W. Chapin of the Boston and Albany Railroad. Gilder forebears and their children had been painted exhaustively by Cecilia Beaux and engraved in bronze by Augustus Saint-Gaudens. My great-aunt Mary O'Hara had written the equine sagas of the Flicka series.

One of the favorite family stories recounted an exploit of my great-grandmother, Helena de Kay Gilder, who was an obsession of the artist Winslow Homer. At her wedding to my great-grandfather, Homer presented to her a special painting. It depicted Helena in a chair, dressed in black. At her feet was a red rose, symbolizing, according to art historians, Homer's heart.

Homer was just one of many artists and writers in my family's circle. My great-grandfather was a close friend to both Mark Twain and Walt Whitman, among many others who visited at our farm in the Berkshires. When Twain's wife died, he retreated to Tyringham and rented from my great-grandfather a house next to ours. But among all the literary figures in the family circle, Helena and my great-grandfather were particularly close friends and backers of Emma Lazarus, the now-celebrated Jewish American poet who wrote the inscription on the Statue of Liberty in New York:

The New Colossus
"Keep ancient lands, your storied pomp!" cries she
With silent lips. "Give me your tired, your poor,
Your huddled masses yearning to breathe free,
The wretched refuse of your teeming shore.
Send these, the homeless, tempest-tost to me,
I lift my lamp beside the golden door!"

In the *Century Magazine*, Richard Watson Gilder published both her poems and her prophetic but sometimes disdained Zionist essays. One of her poems calling for a new homeland was entitled "The New

Ezekiel" and "celebrates," in Esther Schor's words, "the coming together of all the dry bones of Israel":

> Say to the wind, Come forth and breathe afresh
> Even that they may live upon these slain,
> And bone to bone shall leap, and flesh to flesh...
> ...I ope your graves, my people, saith the Lord,
> And I shall place you living in your land.

Prompting the Lazarus poems and essays were the ongoing pogroms in Russia that also inspired "The New Colossus" and brought millions of Jews to the United States. Here they began their relentless rise through all the nation's hierarchies and ladders of accomplishment. Here they challenged all the established powers and principalities.

At the time, WASPs were impregnably on top, running the businesses and media of the day. With notable friendships with two US presidents and such leading lights of literature as Twain, my family was perched near the top of the American establishment. Like most exalted WASP families, my forebears and their descendants were about to face their Israel Test.

Lazarus' biography by Esther Schor is heavily based on hundreds of letters of correspondence between Lazarus and Helena Gilder and reports a suspected romance between Lazarus and Helena's brother, the poet Charles de Kay. By usual standards, my family was actively philo-Semitic. A leading Zionist professor at Columbia told Richard Gilder: "My people owe thanks to you at the *Century* more than to any other publication."

A Tiffany sister of my grandmother was Dorothy Burlingham, the lifetime best friend and collaborator of Anna Freud, daughter of Sigmund, one of the prime forces of modernist Jewish intellect in the twentieth century who revolutionized the treatment of psychiatric illness in children with her own pioneering methods. The tempestuous story of Anna and Dorothy is well told by Dorothy's grandson Michael Burlingham in his book *The Last Tiffany*. On all sides I had relatives with intimate links to Jews.

In our family, however, we were not immune to the general miasma of ambivalent disdain, admiration, and anxiety toward Jews. We took for granted that a person's religion and ethnicity were significant elements of "background." This background stuff was important, and lots of people failed the background test. In describing someone, we regarded their roots to be as worthy of note as their fruits. Jokes about rabbis, priests, and preachers, inflected in rich accents, evoked uproarious laughter around our dinner table. It was another era, I might nervously say today, when one did not consider it offensive to exalt one's own heritage over others or to laugh at ethnic foibles. We were led to believe that our cultural heritage was supreme, and, with some ambivalence, we knew that it had roots entangled in the heritage of the Jews. I suppose we knew also that Jewish intellectuals and entrepreneurs were slowly daring to challenge the preeminence of WASPs in American cultural and commercial life.

Jews were beginning to gain admission into Harvard University in limited numbers, confined by strict quotas that continued into my own era at Harvard in the early 1960s and well into that decade. They exist to this day. As a student at Harvard in the class of 1936, my father roomed with a Jewish classmate named Walter Rosen, who became my own godfather before he, like my father, too, died as a pilot in World War II. Several of my father's other good friends were Jewish. Aunts and cousins married Jews. After graduation, my father visited Germany with another roommate, David Rockefeller, and returned with a passionate revulsion against Hitler's frothing anti-Semitic speeches. My father was convinced that Nazism was a dire threat to civilization and must be stopped by military force.

In 1938, one of the youngest members of the Council on Foreign Relations (to this day the library is named after him), my father famously and impertinently confronted John Foster Dulles, later to become secretary of state under President Eisenhower, for believing that some rapprochement between Germany and the United States was still possible. In sophisticated circles there persisted a fashionable belief, fostered in part by Bloomsbury economist-philosopher John Maynard Keynes, that Germany was essentially a victim of World War I and of the postwar settlement and reparations. There was a notion abroad that Germany had earned by this grievance a moral edge against the winners of that horrific conflict.

My father was having none of it. Based on a conviction that air power would be decisive in the coming war, he took up civilian flight training to be ready while working as an executive trainee at his grandfather's firm, Tiffany and Company. My father died in 1943 commanding a squad of B-17 bombers, called Flying Fortresses, on the way to the war in Europe. The entire squad was lost to what was suspected to have been sabotage at the Gander, Newfoundland, fueling station.

A piano teacher and concert pianist, my mother, Anne, after the war became a close friend of the famed virtuoso William Kapell, who was Jewish, and taught him how to drive a car in the Berkshires, where he practiced his incandescent musical art in a converted red barn next to our house. Only six or seven at the time, I mainly remember how loudly he played compared to my mother. We were all shocked and dismayed by his death in a plane crash in San Francisco while returning from a triumphant concert tour in Australia. When tapes of Kapell's performances in Australia were rediscovered early in this new century, the event was front-page news in the *New York Times*.

Several years younger than my mother, Kapell consulted her about his romantic pursuit of a mutual friend and gave her piano lessons. At the time, he was her favorite pianist, but other Jews soon joined the lists of virtuosi, including Serkin, Horowitz, Rubinstein, Istomin, Fleischer, Barenboim, and Ax, as Jewish genius dominated the global culture of the piano.

On my father's side, Tiffany and Company is no longer independent, having been absorbed by Avon Products, as the "family" jewelry business surrendered to Jewish entrepreneurs, who outperformed the stodgy WASPs in control at Tiffany.

In many walks of life, from finance to higher education, American WASPs have undergone such a displacement. Some are ambivalent about it, but very few in my experience are anti-Semitic, and even those who are anti-Semitic admire many Jews. Nearly all cherish their Jewish friends, associates, and connections. They were proud to have known Henry Kissinger, who became my tutor at Harvard, just as they boast of their youthful encounters with Bob Dylan or appreciate the gifts of Leonard Cohen or Irving Berlin as songwriters. The American economy and culture is not a zero-sum game, and the creative ferment fostered by Jewish inventors and entrepreneurs has enriched the entire nation and made the current generation of WASPs the most prosperous and successful in history. Jews have not only succeeded in America but have saved America as well. They are now so deeply entwined in American culture and enterprise—and in the lives of most Americans—that it is difficult to imagine life in the United States without its Jewish leadership and Jewish accomplishments.

Virtually all Americans who have achieved anything important in the twentieth century have had crucially important Jewish colleagues and collaborators. Virtually none of the significant scientific and technological feats of the last century would have been possible without the critical contributions of Jews. Even some of the best Christian preachers and theologians turn out to have been born Jewish.

As with all nations and cultures faced through history by the plain facts of Jewish brilliance and success, we have a choice. We can either resent it or embrace it as a divine gift to the world. But although our choice is free, the result of our choice is intractably set by the moral law that governs the outcome of human endeavor as strictly as the laws of physics that govern the planets. The envy of excellence leads to perdition, the love of it leads to the light.

Today this choice, with all its relentlessly existential implications, is focused not on the Jews moving into the neighborhood but on the Jews as a nation.

America is a profoundly Judeo–Christian nation, and without the Jewish role, it might well not have prevailed or even survived in its present form. Israel is a national expression of the Jewish genius and achievement that has long been manifest in American life and commerce. We need Israel today as much as Israel needs us, as much as we needed Jewish physicists and chemists, such as Leó Szilárd, John von Neumann, and J. Robert Oppenheimer, to bring to fruition the Manhattan Project that won World War II, as much as we needed Jewish entrepreneurs and inventors to consummate the technologies of Silicon Valley, and as much as we needed Jewish engineers to maintain our national defenses throughout the Cold War and thereafter.

The lesson of the ascendancy of Jews in America is the same as the lesson of Israel today. It is not primarily a tale of sentimental tolerance in which WASP Americans sheltered the needy Jews, but a tale in which America, including American WASPs, incomparably benefited by passing an often brutal and exacting moral test, and accepted, if sometimes grudgingly, the superior performance of another, in some ways, alien people. The point of Lazarus's great poem is not to celebrate America as a vast homeless shelter but as a nation whose genius has been to know that the huddled masses—in their very yearning to breathe free—would surpass all the storied posh and pomp of Europe.

As with America, so with Israel. Israel is not a dispensable Jewish "best friend," a noble but doomed democracy, nor even a charitable dependent we can no longer afford. It is an indispensable strategic ally, and in the past thirty years it has evolved into perhaps one of our most valuable partners.

Yet, for most Americans, ultimately our loyalty to Israel arises not from a cold calculus of survival, but from a sense of the holy. What Americans must fathom with both heart and mind is that this instinct is true—and vital to our survival—that if we would live, we must defend this Holy Land.

INDEX

IBM, 2, 86, 102, 112, 113, 121, 166
Icahn, Carl, 79
ICBMs, 9, 10
Iddan, Gavriel, 108
immigration, 159; Arab, 54, 60, 62; Jewish,
    56–57, 90, 126, 195
imperialism, 2, 18, 44, 133
India, 24, 42, 86, 146
Indonesia, 24, 42
induction, 97
Industrial Revolution, 6, 7
information age, 16, 97–98
information technology, 102–103, 117
innovation, 1, 2, 5, 8, 16, 74, 107, 108, 118, 119,
    127, 128, 189, 190, 195
Inquisition, Spanish, 38, 159
international law, 25
International Monetary Fund (IMF), 65–66
intifadas, 8, 47, 56, 116, 129, 130, 136, 142, 167,
    180; first (1987), 31, 64, 65; second (2000),
    68
IQ, 38, 39, 89
Iran, 10, 27, 49, 77, 136, 143, 159, 162, 166, 168,
    172, 175, 178, 184, 185, 187, 188, 191
Iraq, 10, 54, 55, 56, 57, 127
Irgun, 126–27
Iron Beam, 12. See also laser weapons
Iron Dome, 9–11, 12, 120, 165. See also anti-
    missile systems
Islam, 15, 77, 81
Islamic Jihad, 162
Israeli Defense Forces (IDF), 5, 12, 31, 130,
    160, 178; Sayeret Matkal, 160; "talpions",
    5, 186; Unit 8200, 5
Istomin, Eugene, 202

J Street movement, 154
Jackson, Henry "Scoop", 113
Jacob (patriarch), 138, 147–48, 149
Japan, 2, 8, 49, 83, 95, 125, 181, 188
Jehovah's Witnesses, 37
Jericho, Israel, 52
Jerusalem, Israel, 17, 31, 52, 53, 108, 113, 127,
    130, 134, 135, 136, 138, 146, 149, 161, 180;
    al-Aqsa Mosque, 138; East, 173; Gilo, 129;
    Hebrew University of, 139, 150; Mount
    Scopus, 139; Old City, 134; US Embassy
    in, 4
Jews, 2, 9, 20, 37–38, 43, 46, 53, 55, 60, 65, 66,
    82, 83, 87, 90, 91, 92, 107, 110, 115, 145, 171,
    180, 189, 190, 195, 202; American, 1, 12, 45,
    154, 157, 192, 200–201, 203, 204; expelled

from Arab nations, 3, 31–32, 61, 63, 150,
    174, 175; genius of. See genius; hatred
    against. See anti-Semitism. IQ of. See IQ;
    Israel as homeland for, 21, 54, 56–57, 59,
    111, 126, 183, 185; "New York", 197, 198;
    population of, 12, 17, 173, 184; scientific
    achievements of, 86, 104; Soviet, 113–14;
    wealth of, 23, 32, 41, 71, 78, 79, 80, 196. See
    also Judaism
jihad, idea of, 71, 89, 110, 130, 133, 155, 156, 159,
    171, 172, 180, 189, 191, 192
jihadists, 3, 4, 8, 10, 30, 81, 122, 131, 136, 146,
    166, 167, 168, 176, 179, 180, 181, 184–85, 186,
    187, 188
Jonathan Institute, 155, 161
Jordan (country), 21, 31, 32, 55, 56, 60, 62, 63,
    64, 67, 70, 77, 138, 139, 167, 180
Jordan, river, 27, 33, 51, 63, 67, 71, 157, 173
Judaism, 45, 129, 132, 146; Orthodox, 131
Juneau, Alaska, 154
Justice, International Court of, 27

Kahn, Herman, 151
Kampala, Uganda, 161
Kanaan, Oussama, 65
Kann, Margit, 87
Kapell, William, 202
Karsh, Efraim, 64
Kaufmann, Yadin, 114
Kay, Charles de, 200
Keinan, Tal, 115, 116
Kelvin, Lord, 86
Kemp, Jack, 158
Kennedy, John F., 161
Kennedy, Joseph P., 161
Kenya, 24, 42, 153
Keynes, John Maynard, 202
Khalaila, Razi, 6
Khalidi, Raja, 69–70, 71
Khalidi, Rashid, 59
Kibbutzim, 53, 111
King, Larry, 159
King David Hotel bombing, 127
Kiriath Anavim, Israel, 53
Kirkpatrick, Jeane, 158, 161
Kiryat Gat, Israel, 113, 132
Kissinger, Henry, 168, 203
Klein, Naomi, 25, 41
Klein, Raffi, 112
Knesset, Israeli, 26, 116, 137, 155, 180
Koestler, Arthur, 87
Koren, Guy, 122